EAST ASIAN

Folktales Myths & Legends

EAST ASIAN Folktales Myths & Legends

EVA WONG NAVA

Illustrated by JOCELYN KAO

SCHOLASTIC

Published in the UK by Scholastic, 2024
1 London Bridge, London, SE1 9BG
Scholastic Ireland, 89E Lagan Road, Dublin Industrial Estate,
Glasnevin, Dublin, D11 HP5F

SCHOLASTIC and associated logos are trademarks and/or
registered trademarks of Scholastic Inc.

Text © Eva Wong Nava, 2024
Illustrations by Jocelyn Kao © Scholastic, 2024

The right of Eva Wong Nava and Jocelyn Kao to be identified as
the author and illustrator of this work has been asserted by
them under the Copyright, Designs and Patents Act 1988.

ISBN 978 07023 2523 6

A CIP catalogue record for this book
is available from the British Library.

All rights reserved.
This book is sold subject to the condition that
it shall not, by way of trade or otherwise, be lent, hired out or
otherwise circulated in any form of binding or cover other than that
in which it is published. No part of this publication may be reproduced,
stored in a retrieval system, or transmitted in any form or by any other
means (electronic, mechanical, photocopying, recording or otherwise)
without prior written permission of Scholastic Limited.

Printed and bound in Great Britain by Clays Ltd, Elcograf S.p.A
Paper made from wood grown in sustainable forests
and other controlled sources.

1 3 5 7 9 10 8 6 4 2

This is a work of fiction. Names, characters, places, incidents and dialogues are
products of the author's imagination or are used fictitiously. Any resemblance to
actual people, living or dead, events or locales is entirely coincidental.

www.scholastic.co.uk

*To Claire, who loved stories and Paris –
we will always have Paris!*

CONTENTS

INTRODUCTION — 1

AUTHOR'S NOTE — 9

ORIGIN AND DISCOVERY TALES

Pangu the Giant Creator and Nüwa the Mother Goddess (China)	13
Magohalmi, the Grandmother of Creation (Korea)	25
Shennong, the Divine Farmer (China and Vietnam)	37
Leizu, the Goddess of Silk (China)	51

FESTIVAL STORIES

The Great Race: the Story of the Chinese Zodiac (China, Southeast Asia)	65
The Tale of Nian the Monster (China)	79
Quyuan and the Dragon Boat Festival (China, Southeast Asia)	91

ANIMAL TALES

Sun Wukong, the Monkey God (China, Korea, Japan, Southeast Asia)	105
Mr Mole Finds a Husband for his Daughter (Korea)	121
Crab and Monkey Go to War (Japan)	133
The Not-So-Very-Clever Wolf (Mongolia)	143

TALES OF THE GOOD, WISE AND BRAVE

Kong Rong and the Pear (China)	153
Hua Mulan, the Maiden Warrior (China)	163
Momotaro, the Peach Boy (Japan)	177

ANCIENT LOVE STORIES

Chang'e, Houyi and the Mid-Autumn Festival (China, Southeast Asia)	197
The Legend of Lady White Snake (China)	211
The Butterfly Couple (China, Southeast Asia)	227
The Cowherd and the Weaver Girl (China, Korea, Japan, Southeast Asia)	245

INTRODUCTION

The stories in this book are ages old. As is the case with many ancient tales, we do not know exactly when some of them originated or who first wrote them. What we do know is that they have all been retold through the ages, and they continue to live on in the imaginations of more than one billion people in this world who identify as East and Southeast Asian, and in the minds of those who have chosen to explore these rich folklores.

Who are the East Asians? East Asians are made up of people from China, Taiwan (also referred to officially as the Republic of China), North and South Korea, Japan and Mongolia. Many of the stories in this collection are of Chinese origin. This is in part because they have been well documented and translated over time, whereas others, such as those from Mongolia, have been harder to access due to the scarcity of English sources. Plus, because of ancient political and trade links, Korea and Japan share many stories with China. Many of their old texts were written in ancient Chinese characters, so the stories were accessible to each group of people, but various different versions of the same tales emerged over time. It is difficult to say which versions are the "original" – but this is part of the beauty and nature of folk tales, myths and legends.

Chinese people have also spread far and wide. Many of them left the Middle Kingdom (which is the Chinese name for China, literally translated from the characters Zhōngguó, 中国) during the fourteenth and fifteenth centuries for Nanyang, or the South Seas, the Chinese name for the region south of China that is now known as Southeast Asia. There, they settled in countries like Singapore, Malaysia, Vietnam, Thailand, the Philippines, Brunei, Indonesia, Cambodia and Laos. Because of this migration and immigration, several stories in this anthology are also shared by some of these countries – but it must be said that Southeast Asia as a region is filled with its own unique folklore, fairy tales and myths, which this anthology does not cover.

As time went on, the Chinese headed to all four corners of the world. They left for North America during the nineteenth century in search of gold, to work on the railroads and to escape political turmoil in China. They also went to the Antipodes, especially to Australia, to work in the bush and fields during the late nineteenth century. Chinese communities can also be found in Polynesia, South America, Mauritius, the Seychelles, India and Sri Lanka. While there were already Chinese people in Britain in the nineteenth century, they came in large numbers during the twentieth century when they were invited by the British government to work, study and start families in Great Britain. The Koreans and Japanese have their own migration patterns, with diasporas found in places such as North and South America, Canada and Great Britain. The stories you will read here have migrated with them.

What *all* the tales in this anthology have in common is that they were carried by word of mouth from one generation to another, before they were ever written down. In the old days, when the moon was just high enough in the sky, the village storyteller would announce the story for the evening. The young and old then gathered by the storyteller's feet, eagerly waiting for the tale to begin. Today, storytellers still recite and perform stories to audiences in parts of East and Southeast Asia. These performances are often accompanied by music and singing, like in operas, puppet shows, and plays. In addition, storytelling has gone digital too, and you will find many of these stories adapted into films or animated shorts, including some you may know, like *Mulan* or *On the Moon*.

East Asian mythology contains stories of humans intermingling with gods and deities (shen), animals (dongwu), animal spirits (yao) and immortals (xian). The stories are infused with supernatural magic and mystery.

A number of important mythical characters also find their way into some of these stories: Sun Wukong the Monkey God, the Eight Immortals and Chang'e the Moon Goddess, to name a few. In China, gods are organized in a complex celestial hierarchy called a pantheon, and the Jade Emperor, or Heavenly Grandfather, sits at the top of this hierarchy. The Mongolians, Japanese and Koreans have their own pantheon of gods and goddesses.

These stories are influenced by the folk beliefs, religion and philosophies of the East Asian people – a combination of Taoism, Buddhism and Confucianism, also known as the three teachings. From Taoism, the East Asians understood metaphysics and mysticism. From Buddhism, they learned philosophy and the concept of reincarnation. And from Confucianism, they absorbed rites, rituals, and filial piety and duty – the idea that a good child must honour and obey their parents while they are on Earth and then worship and venerate their ancestors when they ascend to the Heavens and take on god-like status.

Before Buddhism, which was exported to China from India, the ancient Chinese were animists – meaning they saw inanimate objects as possessing life or spirituality: for example, a stone might hold magical powers, or ordinary animals could take on the role of a human. Animists also worshipped the sun, moon and rivers. Later, animistic beliefs came to be known as shamanistic beliefs, and you will see these ancient elements in some of the stories here too.

Although the majority of modern Chinese, Mongolian, Korean and Japanese people are Buddhists, there are also those who had converted to Christianity among the diasporas. Yet, despite the Christian establishment's thinking that these legendary tales of adventure, mysticism and bravery are against Christian beliefs, these tales continue to be shared. Ultimately, they are seen more as traditional stories than strictly religious ones.

The stories retold in this collection were first recounted during a time when girls were often sidelined, when Confucian male-dominated ethics formed the backdrop of East Asian societies and women were considered to be less important than their fathers, husbands and sons. Despite this, the women in many versions of these stories were empowered in their own ways, and often fought against the system that oppressed them. Nowadays, East Asian women may seem more liberated, but they're still living in a patriarchal society, and several of these stories remain relevant today. As for education, few people could read and write when these tales originated. Only wealthy boys and men, aristocrats and those working in the courts of emperors had the opportunity to study. The rest of the ordinary people – men, women and children – worked in fields and workshops. Stories, told in tents, caves, homes and public places, were a way for them to entertain and educate themselves.

For this reason, many of the tales in this book are moralistic – designed to teach children the values of life, how to be good people, and what being great a leader entailed. In this collection of retellings, you get to make up your mind about what lessons these stories are trying to teach, and whether you agree with them. Whatever impression the mystical stories in this anthology may leave on you, it is fair to say that they continue to mesmerize the young and old alike to this very day.

AUTHOR'S NOTE

This anthology is filled with people from the ancient east. Where there are names in Chinese, Japanese and Korean, you'll see that they begin with the family name, followed by the given names, like Sun Wukong. The naming convention in Mongolia differs from the rest of East Asia; Mongolians follow the patronymic system, which traces a person's origins through the father, instead of the family name.

You'll also notice that the names from China, Japan and Korea are written in Roman letters in this book – that is, using letters from the English alphabet. This makes for easier pronunciation. The Romanized names in Chinese are written as they would be pronounced in Mandarin. Mandarin is one of the many Chinese dialects found in China.

Linguists and historians tell us that Mandarin became China's official language in the early 1900s. It is also spoken by many people outside China, such as Singapore, Malaysia and Taiwan. I have chosen to use Mandarin because it is my second language, and one that I know best among the other dialects. In China, Mandarin is known as putonghua, or "common speech", because it is commonly used among the one billion people there. In other parts of the world, Mandarin is known as zhongwen, or "Chinese". There are more than 1.2 billion Mandarin speakers worldwide. This makes Mandarin the most spoken language in the world.

ORIGIN AND DISCOVERY TALES

Every culture and civilization has their own creation myths, offering answers to the great mystery of how the universe began. Discovery myths are also a popular way for people to explore the history of objects and inventions that are most valuable to their culture and society. Here is a group of stories that helped the ancient East Asians in China and Korea understand the origins of herbal medicines, silk and even the world itself.

PANGU THE GIANT CREATOR AND NÜWA THE MOTHER GODDESS

This anthology begins with a Chinese myth about the creation of the universe: the story of Pangu and Nüwa. As with many ancient tales, the origins are blurry, and over time Pangu the Giant's story has been embellished with a variety of different details. It is similar for Nüwa's story, which has many versions – the most famous being the one found in a novel from the Ming dynasty (1368–1644) entitled Fengshen Bang, *or* The Investiture of the

Gods. *The version in this anthology tells us what Pangu did to create the universe and the first humans on Earth, and how Nüwa mended the Sky and created a system of hierarchy in society.*

In the very beginning, there was nothing but darkness. This darkness would become known as the Void. Some people called it the Universe. The Void was a soup of nothingness. Time was never-ending, limitless, and the Earth as we know it did not yet exist.

But even amid this nothingness there was an energy that did not yet have a name. Later, the ancient mystics would call it Wuji, or Infinity. This energy turned and churned in the Void for eighteen thousand years, and finally it created an oval shape: the Cosmic Egg. Within this egg, two powerful opposing forces – Yin-Darkness and Yang-Light – found a way to balance themselves, hugging and becoming one. This force came to be known as Taiji – the supreme, absolute and infinite cosmic energy.

Then, out of this balanced cosmic energy inside the egg, Pangu was formed.

Not long after, the egg cracked open, birthing Pangu into the Universe. He was a strange-looking entity. Pangu was neither man nor beast. His body was covered in a straggly coat of ash-coloured fur. A pair of horns stood out from his head and, beneath a pair of black bushy eyebrows, two bulging eyes stared out into the Void. Above his spongy lips was a moustache that resembled the wings of a blackbird in flight. He had knobbly knees that stuck out from his fur coat, and a pair of huge feet. In his gnarly hands, he held an axe. Pangu was so huge and colossal that the ancient Chinese called him a giant.

As soon as he was born, Pangu started to create the world.

"Haiiiiiii," Pangu said, feet apart, as he raised his axe above his head. "Yaaaahhhhhhh!" he continued, knees bent, as he brought the axe down. The Void shook with the force of his breath and thunderous voice.

With one single mighty swing of his axe, Pangu separated the Universe into two: creating the Earth, which was brown and murky, and the Sky, which was bright and clear. The Earth was given Yin energy, and the Sky, Yang energy. To keep them separated, Pangu the Giant stood between the Earth and Sky. The Earth was firm and flat beneath his feet. But the Sky rested on his wide back, causing him to hunch under its weight.

"Ahhhhhhh!" Pangu heaved, stretching tall. "Hmmmmmm," he grunted, straightening his knees as he lifted the Sky with his broad back, pushing it further away from the Earth.

The Void rumbled as Pangu sighed and grunted. With every day that passed, he stood taller and taller, the Sky grew higher, the Earth became thicker, and the cosmic Yin-Yang energy kept flowing and moving. As the cosmic energy continued churning and turning, new creations began to form and grow.

It was then that Pangu chose powerful beasts and magical creatures to help him: the Qilin, Black Tortoise, Fenghuang and Loong.

The powerful chimera, Qilin, was a magnificent creature to behold. It was a hoofed beast with the body of an ox, horse and dragon, covered in luminous green scales and wearing a coat of fire. Sticking out from his forehead was a horn. Seeing Pangu carry the weight of the world on his shoulders, the Qilin stepped in and offered to give him a rest.

"Qilin, you are kind and wise, embodying all five elements – Water, Metal, Wood, Earth and Fire," Pangu said. "You will help me hold the Universe up, allowing it to grow and prosper, and to keep Fire in control. I will gather others to help us."

Pangu then turned to Xuanwu, the Black Tortoise. Xuanwu had a pair of dragon ears that allowed him to listen to the Universe, and long tentacles stretched from his shoulders and hips. He had a hairy tail that was good for swimming and, like a warrior, he was imbued with the power to endure hardships. During the winter months, Xuanwu would hibernate to gather strength, and in this way he had the capability to live a long life.

"You will be in charge of the northern realm while the east is guarded by the Blue Dragon, the south by the Red Bird and the west by the White Tiger," Pangu commanded Xuanwu. "And, as your element is Water, you will help me to control the seas."

Next, Pangu turned his attention to Fenghuang. This immortal bird was born from the combination of Yin and Yang forces and elements. Fenghuang had the head of a pheasant, the beak of a parrot, the body of a duck and the wings of a swallow. Its legs were those of a crane, and its tail that of a peacock.

"You are the symbol of harmony, and I see the fire in your eyes," Pangu said. "I see how you want to bring about peace. You will help me find balance in Heaven and on Earth."

Finally, Pangu summoned Loong from his abode at the bottom of the sea. Loong had powerful claws and a writhing snake-like body. Like Qilin, Loong held all five elements in his grasp.

"As the one with the authority to control the

weather, Loong, you represent strength and power," Pangu told him. "With the might to overcome obstacles, you will join me in creating a better world. I charge you with the responsibility to control the element Earth."

These four creatures took turns helping Pangu with the Universe, holding up the Sky and balancing all the elements in the cosmos. It is said that together with Pangu, these magical creatures carried on turning and churning the Universe for another eighteen thousand years, after which Pangu passed away. But a powerful source of energy can never truly die, and another energetic entity – Planet Earth as we know it – was formed from Pangu's body.

The Universe momentarily ground to a halt as Pangu's last breath left his body. "This is the world I'll be leaving behind." Pangu whooshed, his dying breath becoming the wind.

Thunder was formed by his rumbling voice. His eyes closed, and the teardrops that formed on his eyelashes became the mist and clouds. His left eye became the sun; his right eye, the moon; and his hair and beard spread across the Sky and became the stars and the Milky Way.

Mountains reached out from Pangu's head, and

from his blood ran rivers. His muscles became fertile land, forests of trees grew from his fur, and his bones turned into the minerals in the soil while his marrow became precious jewels, like jade and emerald. From his sweat came rain to water the forests. Finally, fleas hopped out of his fur and became animals, and some even turned into black-haired humans.

It was said that the Universe continued to churn and turn, expanding and growing, after Pangu's death. The Celestial Heavens came to be populated by all sorts of beings – immortals, gods, demigods, deities and fantastical creatures – and they were ruled by the Jade Emperor, who was the immortal of all immortals and gods, and he came to be known as the first god, or Heavenly Grandfather.

As the ancient sages in the Eastern Seas would come to tell the people, Pangu may have given his life to create the world and populate it with the first humans, but he did not enable them to reproduce, nor did he form a system of rulers and followers among the humans.

It was Nüwa, the Mother Goddess, who made more and more humans to populate the world, and gave them a way to rule over the land and other people.

Sometime after Pangu's death, there was a catastrophic imbalance on Earth. It is believed that this imbalance was due to a celestial battle in the Sky between the water god Gonggong and the deity-emperor Zhuanxu, who was the grandson of the Yellow Emperor, a mythical deity-king. Their feud caused a colossal crack in the four pillars that held up the Sky, which turned the weather on Earth upside down. Fires rampaged, destroying life. Tides caused flooding, ruining rice fields and crops.

It was during this time that Nüwa was born. Like Pangu, Nüwa was neither human nor beast. With the body of a serpent, she slithered about the Earth, witnessing the destruction caused by the rupture in the Sky. She had to find a way to address this imbalance between Heaven and Earth.

Nüwa in her infinite wisdom knew she needed a powerful paste to mend the fracture in the Sky. So, she pounded the five coloured stones to make a paste. These were no ordinary stones, though; they were the five elements: Wood, Fire, Earth, Metal and Water. With this paste, she mended the crack, but it was still not enough, and the pillars, already weakened with age, continued to break.

What I need are four strong legs to hold up the Sky, Nüwa thought. *Where can I find them?*

As she roamed the Sky and Earth in search for these legs, Hailong the Black Dragon woke from his slumber under the sea and caused a huge flood to rise on land. While this drowned out the ravaging fires, gushing water needed to be controlled too, and this gave Nüwa an idea.

"I will travel south to look for Ao, the turtle. A water element like the Black Dragon needs to be calmed by another of his kind."

Nüwa slithered as far as the South China Sea, where Ao had his abode. There, she asked Ao for help.

"Give my legs to you?" Ao asked, incredulous. "Not without a fight!"

And so Ao challenged Nüwa to a duel. Nüwa gathered her strength and won; she chopped off Ao's four legs to create new pillars to hold up the Sky. Seeing Nüwa's power, the Black Dragon retreated to the ocean, and the floods on Earth receded.

With the Sky repaired and the Earth now dry, Nüwa had plenty of time on her hands. She started to feel lonely as she had little company to enjoy the peace that had descended.

"What I need are more people to populate this Earth," Nüwa said to herself.

She pinched a lump of earth, still moist from the flood, and rolled it into a clump of yellow clay. Then she worked and moulded it into a shape that resembled a human. Nüwa rolled another small lump in her palm to make a head, then elongated four small clumps to make two arms and two legs. She wanted her humans to have feet to stand on and hands to work with, and so she created these body parts too. She felt they must have eyes to see, ears to hear with, a nose to smell nature's perfume and a mouth that would be filled with words. Therefore, she gave her figure a face.

When Nüwa was done, she held the shape proudly in the palm of her hand. She blew on it, and the shape came to life. Satisfied, Nüwa continued to make more, and this brought her tremendous fulfilment. Nüwa decided that the shapes she'd created from the yellow-brown clay of the Yellow River and blown to life would become the lords, ladies and nobles of society. They, she said, would be rulers on Earth, since the Sky was ruled by the Jade Emperor.

Nüwa spent days, weeks and months moulding clay into aristocratic people. She made them in various human forms – big and small, tall and short, narrow and broad. Soon, she began to tire from all this activity. She rested for a while and then, when she found her energy again, she plucked strands of her hair and twisted them into a thick cord, which she dragged along the wet earth, forming furrows of clumpy brown mud.

"Aristocrats must have ordinary people to rule. These clumps of mud will become the ordinary people of Earth," Nüwa said. "They will be farmers, weavers, hunters, traders, teachers, and scholars, ruled over by the lords, ladies and nobles made from clay."

When she had created enough different sorts of people, she commanded them to go forth and multiply, and soon the Earth was filled with hundreds, then millions, followed by billions of humans.

And just like this, according to ancient Chinese mythology, Pangu created the Earth and the first humans, and Nüwa populated it with people of all sorts, making some rule over others.

MAGOHALMI, THE GRANDMOTHER OF CREATION

From China, we now travel to Korea to meet Magohalmi, the Grandmother of Creation. Similar to Chinese mythology, Korean mythology is a mix of Shamanism or folk religion, Buddhism, Taoism, Confucianism and local myths and beliefs. The myth of Magohalmi, or Grandmother Mago, has a patchy history, but she is widely credited to have created the world. This is a retelling fusing two stories: that of the legendary Dangun and the mythical Magohalmi.

Over four thousand years ago, according to a Buddhist monk named Il-yeon, an advanced and mighty nation was formed on a body of land surrounded by water. This place became known as Gojoseon, the first kingdom of what was later known as Korea. Located on what is now the border between Korea and China was a sacred mountain, the Baekdu, which still stands today.

It is said that the founder of Gojoseon was a man named Dangun. Dangun came from a long line of male immortals, and he would never have been born if not for his father's curiosity.

Dangun's father, Hwanung, was the son of Hwanin, the Lord of Heaven, and their home was in the Heavens. But Hwanung had a desire to live on Earth. He wanted to live among the trees in the forest, climb the mountains and swim in the sea. He wanted to experience what soil felt like in his hands, the sensation of rain on his face and the shivery coldness of snow on his tongue. He begged his father to send him to Earth.

Being the Lord of Heaven, Hwanin did not understand why his son wanted to be mortal.

"Isn't it better to be immortal and live here in the

Heavens with me?" Hwanin asked. "Here you have servants to take care of you, goddesses that you can choose as your wives, and all the freedom you could ever have from pain and suffering."

But Hwanung's desire was stronger than his father's lack of understanding.

"Abeonim," Hwanung beseeched his father, addressing him in the respectful, formal way, "I wish to know what it feels like to live on that beautiful land below, and I wish to find love and have children of my own. I wish to be different from the rest. Please grant me my wishes, Father."

Luckily for him, Hwanung had a kindly father.

"Go with all my blessings, my son, and start your adventures below. I will give you three thousand dedicated followers so you can live with them on the sacred Mount of Baekdu," said Hwanin.

And so Hwanung went to live below. When he was on Earth, he marvelled at the beauty as far as his eyes could see, and he wondered who had created such a picture-perfect sight. But none of his faithful followers knew.

Hwanung roamed the mountainous peaks of Baekdu, rode on sledges pulled by wild dogs he'd tamed, and lived off the land as much as he could.

Although he had the animals and his followers from Heaven for company, Hwanung started to feel lonely.

One day, as he was out riding on his sledge, a tiger and a bear sauntered past. Sensing Hwanung's celestial presence, they prayed to him, asking that he grant them their wish.

"Can you make us humans, Lord Hwanung?" the bear and the tiger asked. Hwanung understood their desire to be different only too well.

"Take twenty cloves of garlic and this bundle of mugwort," Hwanung told them. "Eat these sacred foods and stay away from the sunlight for one hundred days."

The tiger and the bear accepted Hwanung's gifts with gratitude. However, the tiger gave up after only twenty days. It was unable to stomach any more spicy garlic and bitter mugwort, and staying away from the sun made it miserable.

"I cannot do this any more," the tiger lamented. "It's now up to you, my dear bear."

The bear was saddened that the tiger could not complete its task. But the bear persevered. Hibernating in the belly of a cave had never been a problem. The bear ate as much garlic and mugwort as possible and, heavy with fatigue, it curled into a furry ball and went to sleep. Then, after one hundred days, the bear emerged from the cave as a woman.

She named herself Ungnyeo, which means bear-woman. She was so grateful to Hwanung for answering her prayer that she started to make offerings to him. As time went by, Ungnyeo became lonely. She prayed once more to Hwanung, but this time it was for a son. She also thanked him for looking after her. Hwanung, who was brought to tears by Ungnyeo's devotion to him, decided to marry her.

"Do you know who created this beautiful paradise we live in?" Hwanung asked his wife one day, as they strolled hand in hand in the valley. They were looking for the perfect spot to eat their picnic of boiled rice and pickled cabbage.

"Only a woman can dream up such serenity. Only a woman has the power to bring all the elements together. The creator of our home must be the Grandmother of Creation herself, Magohalmi," Ungnyeo replied in her wisdom.

Her words moved Hwanung, filling him with even more love for her, and he knew that he wanted to share this glorious natural habitat with a family. Soon after, Ungnyeo fell pregnant with their child.

Their son, Dangun, was born when the seasons changed and it was almost winter again: the first human of his kind in Gojoseon, born of a father who was once an immortal and a mother who was once a bear.

Dangun, Ungnyeo and Hwanung lived happily in the valley of Mount Baekdu. It was fertile land that was excellent for planting rice, cabbage and radishes, which were watered by the surrounding rivers and seas. The family never went hungry.

Majestic mountains loomed in the skyline and a sacred bird with a human face, Inmyeonjo, circled the air, connecting sky and land, blessing nature with longevity. The Sam-Jok-Oh, a powerful three-legged crow, resided in the sun that warmed the land; it beamed rays of light, brightening Earth. At night, when the Sam-Jok-Oh slept, the luminous moon peeked out of cloud tendrils, giving the darkness light. A magical turtle lived in the moon; he was known as the Cosmic Turtle and the One-With-Long-Life. These animal spirits blessed the land and the people who lived there.

Each night as she rocked her son to sleep, Ungnyeo spun yarns of tales. She never tired of telling Dangun, who eagerly listened to stories, about how the world was created by Magohalmi, the Grandmother of Creation.

"Before all this splendour, the world was filled with nothing but dark turmoil…

Rumblings woke up Magohalmi, who had been slumbering deeply for many eternities, dreaming of how she could form mountains, valleys, rivers and seas when the time was right.

'Who dares wake me?' Magohalmi thundered.

She did not hear any answer, because the elements were protesting, making loud noises in the dark void of nothingness.

'Who dares to cause such havoc?' Magohalmi boomed.

Again, she did not receive any answer, because the elements were too busy churning chaos.

'What insolence is this?' Magohalmi raised her voice once more.

As before, she was met with no answer but the echoing rumble of chaos.

'It seems that the time is now ripe for me to put an end to all this disturbance. Wood, Fire, Earth, Metal and Water must know where to go and what to do.'

With this declaration, Magohalmi stood up.

Bending her knee, she raised her muscled arms above her head, and stretched as high as she could reach. As she stood, Magohalmi divided the Earth from the Sky. She firmly pushed the Sky upwards to keep it above, and pressed downwards on the Earth with her gigantic feet, making sure it stayed below the Sky.

'Haaaaaah!' Grandmother Magohalmi heaved, as she pushed higher with all her might, ensuring that the Sky was as far away from the Earth as possible. It took her many days, weeks and months to complete this task.

After Sky and Earth were properly separated, Magohalmi realized that her bladder was full. When she emptied it, she caused a huge flood, which became the seas. The rivers and streams inland were formed by the rivulets of water that trickled from Magohalmi. Drip, drip, drip.

'Ahhhh! What a relief.' Magohalmi sighed.

Now that the Earth was filled with water, she thought it was time to create mountains and valleys. She did this by scratching the ground with her thumbs and fingers. She ran her fingers along the Earth and made four lines. These became valleys, surrounded by the mountains she formed by using her thumbs to push the soil into hills. Among these mountains, she hid clumps of ore in the soil. Then she created the forest by ruffling her hands through her hair. The detritus — dandruff and hair — fell to the Earth and became plants and trees.

'What a beautiful landscape I have made,' Magohalmi marvelled. 'And now I must move south.'

She wiped her soil-encrusted hands on her skirt and started to walk. Her skirt swung and swayed, causing chunks of dried soil to fall off. They plopped into the sea, and these lumps of earth became islands, big and small. Then Magohalmi put Fire in a mountain and contained it there. She instructed this element to only show itself from time to time, forming the first volcano."

"Then, what happened, umma?" Dangun asked, waiting for more.

"All this work made Magohalmi hungry. She was so ravenous that she picked up a huge rock and bit into it.

But the rock was so hard. Pffft! She spat the rock out. Bits of pebbly rock sprayed out from her mouth.

Two large boulders followed after. One became the highest mountain in the north of Gojoseon and the other the highest peak in the south.

And that, my son, was how Magohalmi created our world."

"Where is Magohalmi now, umma?" Dangun asked, curious to know what happened to the Grandmother of Creation.

Ungnyeo smiled. "She went back to sleep again to dream up more beauty for our world."

SHENNONG, THE DIVINE FARMER

Thousands of years ago in China, it was not unusual for people to be sick after eating a certain food or drinking from a contaminated source of water. Such was life, and most accepted that they had no control over Fate. All this changed when a special child was born. According to Sima Qian, a historian from the early Han dynasty (206 BCE to 220 CE), this special child was born many millennia ago in the Middle Kingdom. This mythical child had extraordinary powers and went on to become a god-emperor and a cultural hero, respected and venerated for inventing the plough and bringing medicinal plants to the people of ancient China. He became known as Shennong, the God of Farming or the Divine Farmer. In Vietnam, a country that shares certain similar stories to China, Shennong is known as Thăn Nông.

Our story begins in a village surrounded by mountains and rivers. In this village lived the Jiang family. The man of the House of Jiang was the village leader. The land in his village was abundantly fertile, and he grew rice, onions and cabbages, which he distributed to his villagers after keeping enough for himself. His wife was a skilled hunter, who used animal skins, furs and feathers to make the clothes they wore. She was also a talented cook; she trapped animals and caught fish for their meat, using their bones to flavour her soups.

The couple had a son whom they loved very much because boys were believed to be blessings from the Heavens. With a son, they would always have someone to tend their graves when it was time for their bodies to depart the Earthly Realm and their souls to enter the Emerald Gates of Heaven. The Jiang family felt extra blessed because the woman was carrying another child, and from the way the baby moved, she knew it would be another blessing from the Celestial Emperor.

In this village, soups were considered tonics for the body and soul. Drinking broth daily, it was believed, brought good health and longevity. Mrs Jiang made a pot of soup every day for their family dinner. She added the cabbage her husband grew into the earthen pot of bone soup and cooked the rice in another pot with water she collected from the nearby river.

"Mrs Jiang, what is that delicious smell coming from your kitchen?" their nosy neighbour asked one day.

"It's only bone soup, Madam Zhang," Mrs Jiang replied, pleased that Madam Zhang could smell the tonic she was making. Mrs Jiang had added something special into her soup for that night's dinner.

"Ah, you must show me how to make this soup," Madam Zhang said, sticking her head through the Jiangs' kitchen door.

"Of course," Mrs Jiang replied cordially. "Please come in."

Madam Zhang stepped into the Jiangs' kitchen, and Mrs Jiang proceeded to share her recipe with the older lady.

"See this?" Mrs Jiang said, proffering a bunch of green grass to her neighbour. "This is what makes the soup so fragrant."

"This river weed? This is your secret ingredient?" Madam Zhang replied in surprise, giving the verdant bunch a big, suspicious sniff.

The younger woman bobbed her head in excitement.

"It could be a bad grass, younger sister," Madam Zhang warned.

"This grass grows by the duck weeds that we call fuping," Mrs Jiang explained. "Fuping is harmless, so this grass must be harmless too, seeing that it grows so near the fuping."

"Hmm, how do you know it's harmless, sister? Just because it grows next to something harmless doesn't mean it's harmless too," Madam Zhang said, her voice laced with scorn. "You already know how my old husband was so suddenly taken by Yama because of a plant he'd eaten, which we had thought safe."

It was believed that the fallen were taken by Yama, the God of Death. Old Man Zhang passed away shortly after drinking soup that his wife had made with a strange plant with yellow flowers. He had trembled to death, according to Madam Zhang.

"It was bad luck," Madam Zhang continued, refusing to be blamed for her husband's death. "He was fated to go this way. But even so, you mustn't think that your herb is safe."

"Yes, yes, bad luck," said Mrs Jiang. She refused to let another person's bad fortune cloud her culinary prowess. "But this river weed cannot be bad. It's the third time I have used this plant to flavour my soup. Our boy loves it." Mrs Jiang's voice was warmed by the pride she felt for her son.

However, three days later, the boy groaned in pain, clutching his tummy. His brow beaded with sweat and he felt sick in the stomach. Unable to keep it in, he threw up violently into the wooden bucket his mother had placed by his bed. A rash was running rampant on his body as he shook with chills. On the fourth day, his forehead grew hot like the coals his mother lit to cook soup. The vomiting went on for yet another day, until the boy had nothing more to throw up. He lay in his bed, pallid, limp and weak.

"My son." His mother wept in fear. She knelt on the floor and clasped her hands together in prayer. She touched her head to the floor, asking the Celestial Heavens to protect her precious son from the jaws of Yama.

"My boy," his father cried in trepidation. He, too, knelt on the floor, joining his wife in prayer.

Alas! The boy did not last a week. Weakened by the poison that was coursing through his small body, he did not have the strength to battle with Yama.

The Jiang family was bereaved beyond measure.

On the day they buried their son, the baby in Mrs Jiang's belly kicked in grief. Not long afterwards, Mrs Jiang's belly hurt so much that she knew it was time to give birth again.

After a trying time, panting and pushing, Mrs Jiang finally gave birth. It was another boy, just as she had predicted. But the boy did not look like either herself or her husband. Mrs Jiang wept in despair: the baby had the head of an ox and the body of a human.

"Oh, what have I eaten to cause our child to look this way?" Mrs Jiang exclaimed, staring at her husband in bewilderment.

"Don't you see?" Mr Jiang said to his wife. "The gods have blessed us. They have given us a son that is neither human nor animal, but one that is both. This boy will be a god one day."

Indeed, the baby boy had superhuman powers, equivalent to those of gods. After only three days, he was able to speak.

"Baba, Mama, here I am – the son you both prayed for," the boy said, looking up at his parents from his wooden crib.

His parents racked their brains, trying to remember at what point in their lives they had asked for an ox-headed son. But as they looked at their boy, a powerful love filled their hearts and they could only thank the Celestial Heavens for blessing them.

The ox-headed boy fed daily from his mother and within seven days his baby legs grew long and strong. They were so strong that the boy was able to stand up and even take his first steps and start to walk.

His parents then knew that the boy was indeed blessed by the Heavens and the worry on their minds was lightened by this knowledge.

"It is time we named our son, Husband," Mrs Jiang said. "We must name him before his one-month birthday."

"What name should we pick that is meaningful and auspicious?" Mr Jiang asked.

Mrs Jiang thought for a moment, holding her son close to her chest, and then replied, "We should let him choose his name. He knows what he wants to be called."

"I will be called Shinian," the boy replied, looking up at his mother. "It means year of the stone. For a stone is strong and mighty, and this is the year of my birth."

*

When Jiang Shinian turned three, he started to

work the land, helping his father with planting and harvesting. He saw how his father loosened the earth with his bare hands to put a tiny grain into the ground.

There has to be a better way to loosen the coarse earth without dirtying our hands, Shinian thought to himself. *Our hands are good for scooping earth, but what if this scoop was provided by nature instead?* As he thought about this, he was sitting on a tree stump and dragging a stone playfully through the muddy earth. This gave him an idea. He jumped to his feet and loosened the stump from the dirt. He saw how, by moving the tree stump back and forth in its place, the earth around it became softer, looser.

"Father, look!" Shinian shouted out in excitement. "This will help us loosen the earth. I just need to find an animal to pull it for us."

Shinian saw a horse chewing on some hay a short distance away. He slowly crept up behind the horse, so as not to startle it, and brought a rope round its neck before tying that to the tree stump. Then he slapped the horse on its quarters and watched as the animal dragged the tree stump through the earth. In this way, Shinian invented the first plough.

When the soil was soft and loose, Shinian planted

seeds that went on to become the five different types of grains and millet the villagers would eat.

Later, Shinian saw how bodily energy was exerted when heavy things had to be ferried here and there. Men heaved hemp sacks of rice on their shoulders, while women pulled heavy reed baskets of onions and cabbages. Shinian observed how it made them weary and exhausted. So he tamed an ox and harnessed the animal to a wooden barrel with wheels. In this way he invented the cart, which could be used to carry produce. Before this, nobody had ever seen such a contraption.

Shinian was always finding ways to make new things. He tied sharp stones to a wooden handle and made axes. He twisted roots to make strings, ropes and whips. His sense of smell was strong too, and he could tell if a plant was good to eat or bad for the stomach just by using his nose. Shinian sniffed his way through the forest and marshes, smelling and tasting the leaves, weeds and roots he found. He taught his parents what he knew, and they shared what they had learned with the other villagers.

"Madam Zhang, you might want to try this plant, thunder-god vine. Steep some in boiling water to make a tea. Shinian says that drinking this herbal tea will help to take away the pain in your bones," Mrs Jiang told her neighbour. "It has certainly worked for me."

"Ahh, yes, Mrs Jiang, wind is trapped within my old bones, causing my body to ache," Madam Zhang said wearily, taking the generous bag of thunder-god vine back to hers.

"You know, my son is putting all his knowledge in a book," Mrs Jiang said with pride, and Madam Zhang nodded in acknowledgement.

Unlike his parents and everyone else in the village, Shinian had the gift of writing. Every plant that Shinian tasted, he documented. He wrote down their tastes – bitter, sweet, spicy – and how they made him feel. He gave each plant a name. If a plant or root made him feel good, he called them medicines. When something he ate made him feel ill, he noted these down as poisons. Shinian was even able to find antidotes to remove the toxins caused by poisonous plants. He made tea by steeping the good plants in boiling water.

"A poison can be countered by another poison," he wrote in his notes. "There are herbal teas that can cure."

One day, when Shinian was an old man, he came

across a plant that he had never seen before on his usual herb hunt. It was growing on a grassy mound by the river and it had bright yellow flowers. Shinian put the plant to his nose. It didn't smell too bad. He took a little bite, and immediately he felt terrible. Quickly, he jotted down how the plant made him feel. He knew that before he became sicker he needed to go home to brew some antidote tea. He also knew he had the right herbs for the symptoms he was feeling.

But when Shinian arrived home, he wasn't able to brew his tea. He developed cramps in his stomach that were so strong they made him curl into a ball of pain. He became nauseous and began to vomit. In a daze, reeling in pain, Shinian managed to name this plant. He called it *duanchang cao*, which means "break-the-intestine grass". There was no antidote that could save him because Shinian didn't have the time to find one. Like Old Man Zhang, who was killed by the very same plant, Shinian was tragically poisoned by its toxins too.

However, by the time Shinian passed away, he had studied and recorded at least seventy kinds of medicinal herbs. The work he did helped to protect his family, his fellow villagers, and people far beyond

– who all now knew much more about how to farm and how to identify plants that could help or harm them. Because of his contribution to agriculture and medicine, Shinian was elevated to the status of god and named Shennong, which means God of Farming. He is a mythical figure who is still remembered today for helping the people in the Middle Kingdom.

LEIZU, THE GODDESS OF SILK

Leizu is a legendary figure in Chinese literature. The story goes that she was the wife of the mythical Yellow Emperor, the first emperor of the Han people of China, and the woman who discovered silk. This luxurious material was exclusive to China, and its use and production remained China's secret for millennia, until the opening of the first Silk Road during the Han dynasty in 130 BCE. The Silk Road is a network of trading routes spanning deserts and mountains, nations, generations and history – a web of routes that brought silk from China to the rest of the world.

According to legend, in the old days, the Middle Kingdom was ruled by a four-faced emperor known to everyone as Huangdi, or the Yellow Emperor. During this time, the people of ancient China wore clothes that were coarse and rough. When the months were cold and windy, they wore animal skins and fur on their bodies and feet. When the seasons changed and the weather became warmer, they wore clothing made from hemp, a weed with a fibrous stalk that grew abundantly and wildly.

The process of weaving hemp into cloth was long and arduous, and it required plenty of water. Only peasants living near rivers and hemp fields did this job. Hemp could also be used to make ropes and strings because the material was so strong and long-lasting that it could not be easily destroyed. The ancient Chinese wore loose-fitting tunics – long shirts that came down to their knees – and wide-legged trousers, all made from this plant. Even their shoes and the belts fastening their trousers were made of hemp cloth. And because there were no alternatives to this material, even the royalty wore outfits and footwear made from hemp. But Huangdi's wife would change all this.

Her name was Leizu, and she was as beautiful as she was intelligent. Leizu and Huangdi lived in a palace surrounded by fruit orchards that supplied them with apricots, peaches and pears. Proud peacocks strutted about in their garden, which stretched for miles and miles. Fiery phoenixes flew overhead, leaving trails of fire in their wake. Koi swam in the rivers, their golden scales sparkling in the sunlight. Pink lotuses grew from the muddy-bottomed ponds and nodded their heads in the breeze, while peonies grew in rows next to trees laden with plum blossoms.

In this palace, there was a courtyard where a special tree grew. This was the mulberry tree, and the Empress Leizu loved nothing more than to sit under its generous shade to have her cup of afternoon tea, while her sons, Shaohao and Changyi, chased each other happily under the supervision of her sharp eye.

"Don't go too far where I cannot see you, my children," Leizu would call out to them as she sipped her tea, which was made from the leaves of a flower known as the chrysanthemum. The tea was fragrant and soothing, and it made Leizu feel calm.

The empress was mostly content, except for the fact that her tunic and trousers constantly scratched her delicate skin. The coarse fibres caused welts to appear on her arms and legs. Dabbing them with lukewarm chrysanthemum tea was the only way she could comfort her irritated skin.

"Ah, what relief," she would say with a sigh. "If only the gods would grant us the knowledge to make more comfortable clothes."

One spring afternoon, as Leizu was resting under her favourite tree, something that looked like a pellet plopped into her steaming tea. She peered into her teacup and fished out the white plump nut-shaped thing from the bottom.

"Ah, it's hard like a nut. But it's also strangely sticky. I wonder what it is," she said softly to herself.

When she pulled on a fibre sticking out of the nut-like object, it stretched between her thumb and second finger to form a string. She wound the string round her index finger and it stretched longer and longer. She tried to break the string, but it had a resistance to it, even though it was thin and soft.

Leizu held the object to the sunlight and saw that there was a worm growing inside its shell.

"There's a worm cocooned in there. How fascinating!" Leizu murmured.

It then occurred to the empress that this object

must have come from the tree above, because how else would it have fallen into her teacup? She glanced up and saw that her mulberry tree was laden with cocoons of various sizes.

"Quick, guards! Fetch me something so I can climb up my tree," the empress commanded, worried that her tree was being consumed by disease. "I want to take a better look."

Her loyal guards brought a stepladder, which Leizu climbed up to examine the cocoons. She noticed that they rested on leaves that were covered in holes and came to the conclusion that the worms must be feeding on the leaves. She picked a cocoon off a mulberry leaf and inspected it. She looked for a loose string to pull but there was none. Then she had an idea.

Leizu climbed down the stepladder with the cocoon in her hand and asked a servant to bring her a hot cup of tea. When the tea arrived, in went the cocoon. Immediately, Leizu saw white threads pulling naturally away from it. She realized that for the strings to appear, the cocoon must be immersed in hot liquid. *What a rather amazing worm*, Leizu thought.

"I will name this worm *canchong*," Leizu said, as

she sat back down under the mulberry tree. "This little worm's thread will make me the kind of soft clothing I've been praying for."

When the empress returned to the palace, she ordered food to be prepared and tea to be brewed as offerings to Shennong, the Divine Farmer.

"This offering will be made in the moonlight under the mulberry tree," Leizu instructed, and so this became the timing for all future offerings during the Silkworm Festival in China.

After prayers of gratitude had been offered to Shennong, and with the full moon brightly shining above, the Empress Leizu asked for all the silkworms to be picked from her mulberry tree and from every other mulberry tree growing in the palace grounds.

Hours later, her servants brought back bucketloads of cocoons. Leizu examined each one, making sure that the nut-like cocoon was healthy. Then she ordered vats of water to be boiled. When the water was hot enough – *plop! plop! plop!* – she put the cocoons into the water and watched silk threads whirl out. From this, the first silk was produced.

"Thread is no good until it is woven into cloth," Leizu said.

She saw that cloth could only be made by

criss-crossing threads, so she began to experiment. However, it was long, tiring work weaving thread into cloth by hand, so Leizu called for help.

"Craftsmen and carpenters, make me a machine that can weave these threads into a piece of fabric," she ordered.

Doing as she commanded, the craftsmen and carpenters created the first silk loom.

"Cloth is no good until it is made into clothing," the empress said. She used her hemp tunic and trousers as an example, and asked her royal seamstress to make her something similar.

But the royal seamstress had always dreamed of creating more than just a tunic and a pair of trousers, so she went a step further. She made Leizu something more elegant: a robe. This robe was soft and flowed to her toes. It had wide sleeves that allowed for air flow, and a belt held the robe together. It had taken a long time, but now Leizu had her first silk robe. Finally, her skin was not irritated by her clothes.

"Ahhh! This is just wonderful!" The empress sighed, stroking her face with the sleeves. "Simply wonderful. The fabric is so soft and silky."

Leizu showed Huangdi her robe, and when he

held it in his hands, he sighed with satisfaction. Huangdi loved the robe so much that he asked the royal seamstress to make him one too.

"What can we do to make more of these clothes, dear wife?" the Yellow Emperor asked. "From now on, I decree that all clothing must be this soft and silky."

"Lord husband, you must plant more mulberry trees," Leizu said. "The canchong can only grow there, and I have a feeling that, like everything else in nature, there is a season for their birth."

And so Huangdi set about planting thousands of mulberry trees around their palace. When Leizu and Huangdi strolled among these trees, they noticed that during the summer months the silkworms would eat the mulberry leaves, and then at the end of the hot season the female silkworms would leave their eggs on the leaves. These eggs would hatch in spring, producing a worm that formed a cocoon before it finally hatched into a creamy-white moth that fluttered away.

Through numerous experiments, Leizu discovered that silk threads could only be produced when the worm was in its cocoon. But she knew that not every cocoon must be collected. She set about leaving some cocoons to develop into adult silk moths so the cycle could continue.

A pious woman, Leizu knew that it was nature that provided these riches, so she wanted to honour the god who worked closely with Mother Nature.

"Thank you, Divine Farmer, for granting my prayers," Leizu whispered to Shennong.

Every year after this, when it was time to harvest the silkworm cocoons, Leizu and Huangdi, their two sons and their entourage of servants would prepare a feast in honour of the God of Farming, Shennong. Then the harvesting would begin.

When the cocoons were picked and silk threads produced, workers set about weaving thread into cloth. These workers were women who worked day and night to produce the most beautiful material that human hands had ever touched. Soon, Leizu's name spread all over the Middle Kingdom as silk production developed.

But instead of keeping the glory to herself, the wise and gracious Leizu said, "From now on, we will celebrate every woman who weaves silk threads into fabric. There will be a feast in their honour every year."

When Leizu grew old and it was time for her to

leave for the Celestial Heavens, the people of the Middle Kingdom made sure that she would always be remembered. They built a shrine dedicated to her at the top of an ancient mountain that overlooked her beloved mulberry orchard. In this way, every year during a new moon around the month of April or May, villagers gathered during the Silkworm Festival to honour the legendary Empress Leizu, the Goddess of Silk.

FESTIVAL STORIES

This trio of folk tales takes us back to the Middle Kingdom of long ago, when farming and harvesting were the central way of life, when people's destinies were dependent on the whims of nature, and when humans found ways to appease the gods who were believed to live among them. During this time, China was a land of many kingdoms, each ruled by kings and feudal lords vying to rule a united China, and pride for one's nation was considered a virtuous trait. These stories show us how the measuring of time began and introduce two important annual festivals that are still celebrated today – Chinese New Year and the Dragon Boat Festival.

THE GREAT RACE: THE STORY OF THE CHINESE ZODIAC

There are many variations of this story, depending on where it is told and who is telling the tale. It is shared by two countries and their diasporic communities – the Chinese and the Vietnamese. However, it is one of the most widely known East Asian stories, so many people across the world are familiar with the legend of the twelve animals of the zodiac.

Many, many moons ago, when people could not read or write, there was no way to measure time. Days changed into weeks, which passed into months, which turned into years, and years into decades. But the people in the Middle Kingdom did not know this. For them, time was a fluid and never-ending cycle of seasons.

What they knew was that a new season, for which they had no name, began when the weather started to change. And this was when they harnessed their oxen to ploughs so that they could soften the soil to plant seeds for a new batch of crops. If a farmer had no ox, he would use his horse instead. And if a farmer had both an ox and a horse, he would put the two animals to work.

Yong was a farmer who was lucky enough to have both an ox and a horse to pull a plough through his fields. He had two big fields, and the ox worked in one, the horse in the other. When darkness came, and the animals' work was done, they would be brought back to the hut that Yong had built to house them.

Yong was no ordinary farmer. He was an ambitious man who wanted to build a farming empire. He discussed his business plans with his wife, who advised him to buy more animals for their farm.

"Chickens are good for laying eggs, which we can sell at the market," Yong's wife, Fung, said. "And, as there are rats pestering us, we should get cats to help scare these rodents away."

So Farmer Yong invested in a brood of hens and a rooster. He built them a coop inside the hut. He also bought a cat to scare away the pack of rats living under the floorboards of the house.

After some time, Farmer Yong brought a herd of goats to the farm, as goat's milk was nutritious and he could sell the excess.

"Husband, you must now get some pigs because they make for good meat, some of which we can eat and the rest we can sell at the market," Fung advised Yong.

And so Yong bought a drove of pigs. Soon after, the sow gave birth to a litter of pink piglets. This made Yong and Fung very happy. Their farm was thriving and their business was growing.

"Husband, what happens if bandits come and rob us of our fortune?" Fung asked Yong. "We must get a dog to guard and protect us."

Right away, Yong acquired two dogs for their farm, one male shepherd dog and a female of the same breed. These dogs were courageous and protective of their territories, and so he felt that his farm would be well protected. Yong also had in mind to breed some pedigree puppies for sale, as many farmers would want one, or even two, to guard their land. Soon, there was a pack of shepherd dogs on the farm. Yong and Fung loved them all.

"Husband, this is wonderful! Dogs are loyal and lucky animals, and we have a kennel of them that will protect our home and our new baby," Fung said, rubbing her pregnant belly.

"Yes, Wife, but I have always wanted some rabbits to play with. And since our little baby arriving soon, a pet rabbit would be wonderful," Yong announced, and Fung agreed.

And so he purchased a nest of rabbits and built them hutches inside the animal hut. The hut started to get crowded and noisy, and this led to some discontent. The biggest animal living in it was Ox, and he felt that he should be given more respect, since he was bigger than Horse. But Horse felt he should be the leader because he was stronger than Ox. The two animals bickered constantly.

"Neighhhhhh, I am the boss," Horse said.

"Naahhhh, I am the boss," Ox argued.

Their quarrels made living with them unbearable for Dog, Cat, Rabbit, Goat and Rooster, who, being smaller animals, wanted their families to live in peace and tranquillity under one roof. Even though he had been brought in to scare the rodents, Cat often left Rat alone, since there was nothing Cat liked to do better than nap. Chasing Rat was simply too tiring for him. Rat was the tiniest of all the animals, and he just wanted everyone to get along.

As this noisy chatter was going on at Yong's farm, there was a cacophony in the jungle not far away too. Tiger was prowling and growling in dissatisfaction. He felt that nobody paid him any respect at all. No animal seemed to fear him, and he did not like that. Instead, they seemed to be scared of Snake, who slithered on the ground.

"What a lowly creature Snake is," Tiger grumbled. "And they are afraid of him? Grrraaahhh!"

"Who are you calling lowly, Tiger?" Snake sneered. "You may have stripes and walk on four legs, but I have venom that would kill you in an instant."

Tiger made sure to stay away from Snake, and Snake teased Tiger with her two-pronged tongue and bared her fangs at him. "One bite, Tiger, one bite," Snake would hiss relentlessly.

"I am still bigger than you, silly old Snake!" Tiger taunted as Snake slithered away.

At that moment, Monkey scampered by and screeched at both Snake and Tiger for being so ridiculous.

"I am the leader, of course!" Monkey said. "With my prehensile tail that clings on to branches as good as any fingers and thumbs, and which enables me to pick up fruits, *I* am the best in the animal kingdom."

Another season passed and the noise of the animals bickering on Earth grew louder and louder until it reached the ears of Jade Emperor in the Celestial Heavens.

"What is this racket?" Jade Emperor asked in annoyance. "Why are all these animals making so much noise that even the Heavens are disturbed?"

He peered down at Earth from his celestial palace and saw Yong ploughing the land with Ox pulling the plough, while Horse was haughtily whinnying at Ox from the other field. Because humans do not understand animal talk, the farmer was clueless about what Horse was saying. But Jade Emperor heard Horse telling Ox that since he was able to run faster, to gallop and canter, he was better than Ox, and should be the leader of all animals.

Now, Jade Emperor, being the Supreme Ruler of the heavenly skies, did not like what he was hearing. "What is this nonsense? *I* am the leader of all animals and humans. I must do something to stop this silly and unnecessary bickering."

Jade Emperor then summoned his ministers and advisers to ask them for ideas. But none of them could tell him what to do.

"Oh, for the sake of feathering pheasants! I must think of a plan," Jade Emperor said as he paced his gigantic palace day and night.

The emperor's pacing agitated Dragon, who was fond of his master. "Why fret, my honourable emperor? Why not get all the animals to enter a race to compete for their leadership positions?"

"What a brilliant idea of mine that you're voicing, Dragon!" Jade Emperor clapped his hands in delight. "You are indeed a clairvoyant, reading my mind like that."

Dragon yawned and picked his teeth with his sharp claws. "Of course, my highest emperor, of course! And while you're at it, why not teach your humans to tell the time as well? Look at Farmer Yong. He can't tell the difference between night and day, nor between summer and winter, spring and autumn. To him, time is merely a temperature change, and he sleeps when he's tired and eats when he's hungry. He needs a better routine. In the process, you could give each animal something to be proud of. Make them the leader of time in a yearly cycle."

"Now, there was something else I wanted to do," Jade Emperor said thoughtfully, as he stroked his long silver beard. "It's not too late to regulate the Middle Kingdom into different times and seasons and give humans words to describe time. I will divide time into twelve months, which will make one year, and each year will be presided by an animal. I will organize a race to decide who'll be the first animal. That animal, the first to cross the line, will be leader for a whole year, followed by the next animal and the next. Dragon, what do you think of my brilliant idea?"

"Your idea, my lord emperor, is as brilliant as mine!"

So Jade Emperor rode on his celestial cloud and flew down to Earth.

"Hear! Hear! Animals of the Middle Kingdom!" Jade Emperor boomed. "I am organizing a race. This race will take place at the river by the jungle, and whoever crosses the river first will be the leader of

Time. It is also my birthday today, and because of this I will be most generous."

The animals at the farm were excited beyond words, Ox more delighted than most. The animals in the jungle were equally animated, Tiger being the most thrilled. Now he could at last show his prowess and power. But not all the animals on Earth were interested. So, on the day of the great race, only thirteen turned up: Ox, Horse, Cat, Rat, Pig, Dog, Goat, Tiger, Monkey, Rabbit, Rooster, Snake and Dragon who flew to Earth with Jade Emperor.

"Ah, there are only thirteen of you?" Jade Emperor said, hiding his disappointment. "Never mind. The race will begin even so."

There was a kerfuffle on the riverbank as the animals readied themselves for the race.

"Ready, steady... On your marks, get set – GO!" Jade Emperor commanded.

Ox lumbered and waded into the river. Horse galloped right in, treading water with his front and hind legs. He neighed at Ox just as Cat and Rat jumped on to Ox's broad back to get a ride.

"Get off, you lazy pair," Ox said, trying to shake them loose. But the two animals clung on, Rat holding steadfast to one of Ox's ears, and Cat to the other.

Pig, Dog and Goat decided to share a raft to cross the river. "Teamwork is better than no work," the three animals said in unison.

Tiger leaped from out from behind a huge redwood tree and Snake slithered closely behind him, and both animals took their places next to Horse in the river. Being a giant cat, Tiger did not love the water, and he side-eyed Cat, who'd had the great idea to stay dry by clinging to one of Ox's ears. But Tiger was determined to show everyone he could swim.

Monkey observed this from her place next to Rabbit and Rooster on the riverbank. Then she swung from branch to branch in the trees overhead, finding a way to cross the river. Meanwhile, Rabbit leaped from river stone to river stone. Everyone knew that chickens could not fly, but this did not stop Rooster from trying. He flapped his wings and flew little by little across the river, resting on boulders whenever he had a chance.

Jade Emperor watched closely, and he saw how each animal differed one from another in their characters. Ox, he noticed, was strong but stubborn. Horse was energetic but proud. Jade Emperor noticed the intelligence and wit of Monkey, who found a way to cross the river without getting wet. The Celestial

Ruler observed that Rat had soft skills that Cat did not. In this way, he took heed of all the animals' strengths and weaknesses.

Ox had almost reached the other side when he swung his head sharply to get rid of some pestering mosquitoes, and a loud MEOW was heard. Cat had fallen into the river.

"Help me!" Cat said, mewling at Rat, who he thought might be friend enough to come to his aid.

But Rat ignored Cat and urged Ox to hurry up – then just before the crossing line, Rat leaped from Ox's back and crossed the river first. Huffing, Ox reached the bank next, which made him second in the race.

Tiger swam into third place, followed by Rabbit in fourth – though she could have been third if she had not wasted time trying in vain to help Cat.

Snake was about to finish after Rabbit when Dragon suddenly decided to join the race with the earthly animals. He swooped in, beating Snake to fifth place. Snake was cross, coming in at sixth place.

Horse trotted in at seventh, and behind him came Goat. How Goat finished eighth when he had been on the raft alongside Dog and Pig was a wonder. Both his friends had thought Goat hated the water, but they were obviously mistaken, because as they neared the finish line Goat jumped into the river and swam the rest of the way to shore.

Monkey swung in at ninth place, and she was satisfied with her feat. Rooster flapped his wings and hopped on to the opposite bank at tenth, only slightly wet. And, finally, the raft touched the shoreline just in time for Dog to bound out at eleventh, followed by Pig, who was the twelfth and final animal to cross the river.

The excitement was infectious, and during the announcements declaring each animal's place in the ranking, nobody bickered and fought, as everyone knew they had earned their places.

"As time is never-ending," Jade Emperor declared, "I will make one year twelve months long in honour of you all, the twelve animals that took part in the race. Then each of you will take your place as leader for one whole year, starting with Rat!"

As all this was happening, Cat, who had of course been rudely thrown into the river and lost the race, slunk away to Vietnam to be as far away from Rat as possible.

From this day forward, the bickering between the animals on Earth eased, and farmers in China had names for the seasons and the weather. What's more, the people of the Middle Kingdom celebrated each new year led by a different animal, a practice that still continues today.

And in Vietnam, which is not far from China, the people celebrate the Year of Cat instead of the Rabbit – but they love Rabbit just as much, because she had tried to help Cat.

THE TALE OF NIAN THE MONSTER

This story is an important piece of Chinese folklore. For more than three thousand years, versions of this tale have been retold each year on Chinese New Year. During this festival, many Chinese people say 'Guo Nian', which means to cross over to the new year. It also means to overcome Nian, and this saying is rooted in the following legend about a monster known as the Nian Shou, who had to be defeated so that everyone could celebrate the new year in peace.

Long ago, in a land where mountains peeked out from clouds and a river with water the colour of turmeric flowed into the Yellow Sea, there was a very wise and brave woman.

Lao Niang lived alone in her humble wooden hut on the edge of a village at the foot of a mountain. She had built this home herself, being unmarried and with no male relatives to help her. Lao Niang never complained and was always grateful for whatever the gods bestowed upon her. She knew that the gods had the power to grant humans good fortune and good health. With this knowledge, and to ensure that she stayed in the gods' good favour, Lao Niang always gave daily thanks to the most important god of all – the Celestial Jade Emperor, Ruler of all Heavens, Earth and the Underworld. Though because the old lady believed in being fair, she also paid homage and respect to Tianhou Mazu, the Goddess of the Seas and Heavens.

Lao Niang's daily rituals consisted of prayers and food offerings. To the Jade Emperor, she offered sweet sticky-rice cakes and steamed buns. When pomelos and pears were in season, she made sure that the Jade Emperor had his fill. What he could not finish she ate up, because Lao Niang knew that if one wasted not, one wanted not.

For Tianhou Mazu, Lao Niang prepared vegetable and meat stews, as well as a platter of various fruits, because she knew this was what the Empress of the Heavens loved. Again, she would eat up what the goddess could not finish.

Lao Niang also lit fragrant incense and red candles, and she kept their shrines clean. As she could read and write, which was a rare thing in ancient China, she composed a rhyming couplet on red parchment each day, just like her father had taught her when she was a little girl, and pasted the paper on the door jambs of her home.

"For good luck," Lao Niang whispered as she removed yesterday's paper and stuck on a new one. "Oh, bless this home and village, honourable Celestial Ruler and blessed Tianhou Mazu, Empress of the Sea and Heavens."

The village Lao Niang lived in was very small, with only twelve houses, but she was beloved by all her neighbours because she was a kind woman. When she had extra steamed buns, she gave them away to the village children. Each year during the new moon, she made a sticky-rice dessert, which she called *niangao*, new year cake, and gave each household one to celebrate the new year.

But one day disaster struck this small village. On the eve of a new moon, just before the start of the new year, a monster appeared as if from nowhere. Water dripped from his mane, and saliva from his sharp fangs. A pair of menacing horns stuck out above each eye, and a long one, like a sharp spear, grew from the middle of his head. His body was covered in shimmering venomous scales, and his long tail whipped the air in fury.

When Lao Niang set eyes on this monster from the safety of her hut, she knew that the villagers were doomed, for the monster's eyes reflected nothing but destruction and death. Just as she had thought, the monster proceeded to devour the livestock that were kept at the edge of the village and almost every living thing – crops and plants, the grains and wheat – that the villagers had to eat, until there was nearly nothing left. Then Lao Niang noticed how the monster eyed the children greedily.

"Quick! Hide your children," Lao Niang warned the villagers at the top of her voice, "before the Nian Shou gobbles them up too!"

The children – who had been playing joyfully and hadn't seen the Nian Shou – were gathered and taken quickly indoors as the monster prowled the village. Homes were boarded up and doors barricaded as the monster rampaged outside, destroying everything in his way.

The next day, on the first day of the new year, the villagers opened their doors to an eerie silence and a sorrowful sight. Oxen blood pooled in puddles everywhere and feathers littered the paths along with bits of cabbage leaves. The few chickens and ducks that had escaped the Nian Shou's jaws wandered amid the debris, lost and dazed. Hens clucked for their chicks, and confused ducklings who had lost their parents quacked back in reply. The Nian Shou's gigantic footprints were imprinted into the muddy ground and the villagers could see just how enormous the beast was from the size of his paws alone. That new year's morning, instead of celebrating, they sobbed in despair.

Lao Niang encouraged her friends and neighbours to start all over again. She helped them gather the surviving animals and rebuild the coops to keep their chickens and ducks. An ox was found wandering some miles away and brought back to the village so that land could be ploughed and crops regrown.

Lao Niang handed out her usual niangao, which cheered the villagers up a little. Each of them ate their new year cake with gratitude but also fear. Would the Nian Shou come back again? Nobody could tell, but everyone knew that they had to be prepared.

Life in the village slowly went back to normal, and for a whole year there was peace. A new baby was born, and the villagers celebrated this good omen. Soon, it would be the new year again, and Lao Niang started to make her niangao in preparation. This year, the villagers brought their livestock into their homes, just in case the Nian Shou returned. Lao Niang decided to leave a new year cake outside her front door to appease the monster.

"Eat this instead of our animals," Lao Niang said, hoping that the spring breeze would carry her words to the Nian Shou.

As the new moon appeared high in the sky, a rumbling noise could be heard. It was the Nian Shou, returning for his yearly feast… But when he reached the village and saw that there was nothing for him, he howled so loudly that the villagers cowered in terror inside their wooden homes.

The beastly monster's angry howls were accompanied by a fearful cry from Mrs Li from across the street, who could not find her son. Lao Niang peered through the cracks of her boarded-up window and saw the Nian Shou baring his teeth, sniffing for food. Then, to her horror, she spotted her neighbour's missing boy playing outside. The Nian Shou had seen him too and was now watching the toddler crawling across the ground.

Lao Niang knew that she had to think on her feet as the boy's life was in danger. With sticky saliva dripping to the ground, the Nian Shou looked as though he was going to gobble up the poor child at any minute. Lao Niang grabbed two saucepan lids from the kitchen table and strode quickly and bravely out of her front door.

"Aye, Nian Shou!" Lao Niang shouted, banging the two lids together like cymbals. "Aye, over here!"

Clash! Bang! Clang!

The noise was enough to get the Nian Shou's attention. He turned to peer at Lao Niang. She clapped the lids in front of the monster's face, and this time the Nian Shou shrank back and sat on his haunches, cowering in fear. He looked wildly about as if searching for somewhere to hide.

"Haaaah! He is afraid of loud noises," Lao Niang said quietly to herself. Then she stood up taller, banging her pot lids loudly, and shouted, "Take your baby indoors, Mrs Li!"

Clap! Bang! Crash!

The Nian Shou backed away at the ruckus. Then Lao Niang saw a new flicker of fear in his eyes. In the reflection of his gigantic pupils, she saw what the Nian Shou was looking at: the red paper couplets pasted on her door frame.

"Ohhh, he must be scared of red!" Lao Niang said to herself.

She ran indoors to retrieve her long red scarf. She wound it round her neck and stepped outside again. When the Nian Shou saw Lao Niang in her red scarf, he backed away instantly. Lao Niang stamped on the ground, one foot at a time, and flailed her arms about, acting like an angry ox about to charge. The monster gulped and yelped in terror.

The neighbours, peeking out of their windows, had seen the courageous Lao Niang banging the lids of her cooking pots and heard her shouting at the Nian Shou, and now they came out in droves and walked towards the monster. One woman struck two wooden sticks loudly together and he trembled. Her daughter clapped her hands at the Nian Shou and he shuddered. One man carried a flaming torch and jabbed it towards the Nian Shou, which made the beast turn round and run back to his lair, tail between his legs.

"The beast is afraid of fire," Lao Niang said, and, with a cheer, she continued. "Be gone, you terrible beast! No awful monster can ruin the new year."

Then to the villagers, she said, "The Nian Shou will never terrorize us again, because he is a coward, and we have overcome him! Now we can forget the old year, which was full of fear and bad luck, and cross over to a new one filled with hope and prosperity."

After this, Lao Niang gave thanks to the Jade Emperor and Tianhou Mazu for the courage they bestowed upon her.

"Thank the Sky, thank the Earth and thank all Heavens above," Lao Niang chanted as she lit three incense sticks and bowed in gratitude to the gods. "Protect us always from this terrible beast." She also offered the Jade Emperor and the Empress of the Seas and Heavens a niangao each.

From that day onwards, the villagers knew exactly what they needed to do just before the start of each year, on the eve of the new moon. They would make lots of noise, by hammering their pot lids and cooking utensils, write many good-luck couplets on red parchment to decorate their homes with, and even wear the lucky colour red to ring in the new year. They would also thank the Heavens for helping them cross over to the new year, and remember the bravery of Lao Niang by making and eating niangao. Soon, the whole Middle Kingdom followed in the footsteps of Lao Niang, who saved the new year for everyone in her village and the villages beyond.

As the people prospered and multiplied, they shared these festive rituals and traditions with their friends, family and distant relatives. Many generations later, when gunpowder was invented, people made firecrackers that popped and banged, imitating the sounds that Lao Niang had made with her pot lids to scare away the Nian Shou. And even more generations later, when the people of the Middle Kingdom started to travel and move to new countries overseas, they took their traditions and rituals with them. They never forgot how an old lady named Lao Niang was brave enough to save the new year for everyone.

QU YUAN AND THE DRAGON BOAT FESTIVAL

The Dragon Boat Festival, or Duanwu Jie, is celebrated annually by many Chinese people worldwide. It takes place on the fifth day of the fifth lunar month, between late May and June, and it is marked by dragon-boat racing and eating zongzi – savoury meat-filled rice dumplings. The Dragon Boat Festival is celebrated in memory of a patriotic poet, Qu Yuan, who is remembered for his contribution to the first volume of Classical Chinese Poetry, known as the Chu Ci, or Songs of Chu.

His story is set during the Warring States period (476

to 221 BCE), a time of great division in the history of ancient China, when small kingdoms were warring with one another. It was also a time when feudalism was at its height, which meant that the wealthy nobles, who were favoured, were granted plots of land by the king to build palaces and mansions and they were given poor servants, called serfs, who had to work the land and serve them.

According to the Great Historian Si Maqian, who lived during the Han dynasty, a baby boy was born around the year 340 BCE into a noble family in the state of Chu. His parents named him Qu Yuan. He was a curious boy with an agile mind, and he loved words, especially when they were lyrical and rhyming.

Every night, his scholarly father would recite a poem to him; the ones that excited Qu Yuan the most were the poems that spoke about love for one's country and the valour of those who honoured their king and state. These odes to patriotism, many written by unnamed poets, inspired Qu Yuan to do more for the state of Chu.

During Qu Yuan's youth and adulthood, the state of Chu was at war with the neighbouring Qin state. Corruption was rife, but Qu Yuan's father instilled in his son a sense of justice, propriety and integrity.

"Never succumb to corrupt ways, my son! Greed and dishonesty are maggots that eat away at men's souls and a nation's stability," the older Qu said to his son.

The state of Chu was in the central valley of the river Yangtze, and the water of its tributary, the river Miluo, flowed directly into the Yangtze. Qu Yuan loved taking long walks along the Miluo.

The Miluo was more than one hundred and fifty miles long, and in its waters golden carps, pets of the water goddess Shuimu Niangniang, could be seen swimming in and out of weeds. As a young boy, Qu Yuan would chase frolicking dragonflies, his favourite insect, along the Miluo's banks and dip his toes into the cool water during the hot summer months. When he cupped his hands to take a drink of the Miluo's water, it tasted sweet and refreshing.

As a teen and young adult, it was by the Miluo that Qu Yuan would reflect on the many things in life that interested him, as well as those that bothered him. Walking in nature also inspired his poetic imagination, and he would rush home to pen them with his calligraphy brush. Writing poetry helped Qu Yuan to express his thoughts and clear his mind.

One day, Qu Yuan arrived home from his invigorating daily walk to find his father shaking his head in despair, brows furrowed in consternation. Qu Yuan had noticed that his father had been frowning a lot lately.

"Father, what disturbs you?" Qu Yuan asked.

"Our country is slowly being eroded away by the King of Qin. He has plans to form one big nation and to rule it all, and it saddens me to know that one day our kingdom of Chu will no longer be."

"Father, there must be something that can be done. All the warring states are vying to rule the Middle Kingdom, and Chu stands as good a chance as any."

"Our ministers are all corrupt and untrustworthy, my son – each man for himself. To build a nation, great sacrifices need to be made. One must be able to give up the self for the nation."

A few days after Qu Yuan's father said these words, he passed away, a broken-hearted man. Qu Yuan was by then a man of twenty. Determined to right the wrongs his father saw in the state of Chu, he decided to become a politician. He applied to the Chu government for a position in the courts, and after many rigorous exams Qu Yuan was appointed as an official serving King Huai of Chu. The eager Qu Yuan immediately started to learn about his role and, with great fervour in his heart, he did his best to ensure that no corruption was committed under his watch.

Soon, Qu Yuan's no-nonsense, straight-talking personality became known to King Huai. The king praised Qu Yuan for his good work and promoted him to Left Minister and the Minister of Policy and

War. But there was nothing that Qu Yuan could do to prevent jealous and sycophantic ministers from slandering his good name and whispering into the ears of King Huai, changing the mind of the king against Qu Yuan.

"My Lordship, you must be careful of this man named Qu Yuan," said the Minister of Rivers and Forestry. "No man who chases dragonflies can be trusted. I've seen him by the Miluo river. He acts like a child."

"Your Excellency King Huai," said the Right Minister who was also the Minister of Education and Culture, "Qu Yuan does nothing but pen poems in his free time. Surely that is not an appropriate pursuit for an official, being that he is also the Left Minister and Minister of Policy and War?"

King Huai listened intently to both these ministers and then he called a meeting with Qu Yuan. He demanded that Qu Yuan explain to him his strategies for stopping the feuds that had been going on for many, many years. Qu Yuan was honest and told King Huai that it would be wise if he did not further agitate King Huiwen of Qin. Now, King Huai did not like to hear this, as he considered it insolent of Qu Yuan to suggest that it was he, King Huai of Chu, who was causing a rift between Chu and Qin, when he was convinced it was really the arrogant King Huiwen who was the menace.

"What a preposterous thing to say, Minister Qu Yuan! As my subject, aren't you meant to support me? As King of Chu, I have the power to behead you, but instead I order you to be banished from this state. You shall serve me in exile north of the Han River and you will only report back to me when I command you to."

Devastated, Qu Yuan left his home state as instructed. He lived for many years near the river Han, which was on the other side of the Great Yangtze, feeding into the Yangtze from the east. There, he penned poems that reflected his emotions. He felt abandoned by his king, and he was utterly downcast when he heard news about what was happening to his beloved kingdom. He felt helpless as the bigger and mightier Qin state encroached deeper and deeper into Chu.

When things could not get any worse, Qu Yuan was suddenly summoned back to Chu. By that point, King Huai had passed away after being held captive by the Qin, and his son, King Qingxiang, was on the throne. A stirring in the state of Qin needed to be dealt with, and this compelled the new Chu king to summon Qu Yuan back. King Qingxiang felt that he was the best man for the job, since many of Qu Yuan's supporters had managed to finally persuade the new monarch to bring the poet back home.

However, before Qu Yuan could do his job, another scandal broke out in the court of Chu. Qu Yuan's name was maligned by jealous ministers again, and he was exiled, this time to the regions south of the Yangtze River.

Although he felt betrayed once more, Qu Yuan spent his time in exile collecting regional legends and folklore, documenting the stories of the land and its people. It has been recorded that Qu Yuan also practised shamanism during this time, communicating with spirit-gods, learning from their wisdoms and telling them of his woes. As a man who loved classical literature, he began to study and rewrite ancient poems, and even wrote many of his own, expressing his deep emotions and concerns for his nation state of Chu.

Qu Yuan did manage to return to Chu. But by this time he was an old man, and a very disappointed and depressed one. His mental health had suffered from constantly worrying about his home state. To calm himself, he once again took long walks along his favourite river, the Miluo. During this time, he was mostly alone in his thoughts and anguish. His friends, who loved him, could do nothing to help Qu Yuan, even though they would accompany him on these walks every now and then.

One day, the fifth day of the fifth lunar moon, the wife of one of Qu Yuan's friends made some sticky-rice dumplings and, knowing how Qu Yuan loved them, his friend wanted to share them with him.

"Brother, I have some delicious zongzi to share with you," the friend said cheerfully, knocking on Qu Yuan's door. "These are the ones that you love, filled with savoury meat and sweet chestnuts. Let's eat them while they're hot."

But Qu Yuan was not at home. Knowing where Qu Yuan would be, the friend went to the Miluo in search of the poet. He must be either taking a walk or having a swim in the river. But Qu Yuan's friend was unable to find the poet, even after walking the length of the long river and back.

It was almost dusk by the time Qu Yuan's friend spotted a dragonfly, which led him to a fishing boat moored nearby. He rowed the boat to the middle of the Miluo in search of Qu Yuan. But, alas, there was no sign of him.

The friend then organized a search party, and people came out in groups to look for the missing poet. They walked the Miluo, carrying lanterns, and rowed in its water, calling out the poet's name. Some even threw rice dumplings into the river, asking the water goddess Shuimu Niangniang for help to find Qu Yuan. The search went on for many days and nights, but poor Qu Yuan could not be found.

"I'm saddened that our friend is missing. He has done such great work for his country and people. We must honour his memory," one of Qu Yuan's friends announced.

"Because Qu Yuan penned his thoughts and feelings in an epic poem, 'The Lament', there is historical evidence to show that what the kings of Chu did to Qu Yuan was real," another of Qu Yuan's friends said.

"The story of Qu Yuan might not be a happy one, but we must still share it with our children and grandchildren, because an honest and upright man like Qu Yuan cannot be forgotten," yet another faithful friend insisted.

In this way, Qu Yuan's loving friends and supporters ensured that the story of his mistreatment and the memory of his good deeds and values were passed down from one generation of Chinese people to another. For close to 2,400 years, the spirit of the patriotic and poetic Qu Yuan has continued to live on. Every year, billions of Chinese people and those with Chinese ancestry gather with their friends and family to watch dragon-boat races and eat delicious zongzi in commemoration of him.

In the nation of Taiwan, he has been immortalized and given the status of a water god, known as one of the Shuixian Zunwang, or Eminent Kings of the Water.

ANIMAL TALES

In the folktales of countries like Japan, Korea, Mongolia and China, anthropomorphized animals have long entertained and educated the young. They are often used to represent human traits that are considered ideal and aspirational – or the opposite. In this quartet of stories, you will find an array of animal characters with human qualities. Some are witty, kind and intelligent, while others learn the error of their arrogant, foolish or cruel ways through a tough lesson.

SUN WUKONG, THE MONKEY GOD

Sun Wukong is the most beloved and famous mythical animal-god in Chinese folk and literary culture. He is renowned for his supernatural powers, mischievous antics and magic. Sun Wukong's adventures were compiled in a novel from the Ming dynasty (1368 to 1644), Journey to the West, *attributed to Wu Cheng'en.*

Journey to the West is an epic work of fiction, filled with fantasy and magic, immortals and gods, emperors and ordinary folks, and characters both real and mythological. It is set in two realms – the real world and an imagined one. The novel is both a literary and humorous masterpiece, mixing religious philosophy with satirical slapstick, and it has been adapted to entertain children and adults alike from the east to the west since the sixteenth century.

Sun Wukong is loved by the Chinese diaspora all over the world for his attempts at self-cultivation – perfecting the imperfect self – a Confucian ideal to which East Asian people in general aspire. He is especially beloved in Taiwan, Singapore and Malaysia, where he is sometimes referred to as the Monkey God, with temples dedicated to his worship. In Japan he is Son Gokū, in Korea he is named Son Oh Gong, and in Vietnam he is Tôn Ngộ Không.

In this adaptation, we learn about how this animal-god came to be named Sun Wukong, and why he was banished by his master, the immortal Subodhi, from the Holy Wutai Mountain.

Once upon a time, on the eastern continent, in the land of Aolai, there was a mountain called Huaguo Shan that was abundant with flowers and fruits. At the very top of Huaguo Shan, there sat a giant rock. It was white and smooth like a duck's egg, and it glinted in the light radiating from Taiyang Gong, Grandfather Sun. When the moon appeared at night, the Moon Goddess, Chang'e, would shine on the rock, enveloping it with her glow. When the wind blew, the rock swayed gently back and forth, like a baby cradled by its mother.

It must be said that this was no ordinary rock. Inside the rock was a stone egg, and within this stone egg, a stone monkey slept. When it was time, the rock cracked open, and the stone egg fell out of it. Stroked by the easterly wind, Stone-Monkey burst out from the egg triumphantly, and the air crackled with divine magic. He stood tall and proud and surveyed the land before him.

"I am born!" he announced confidently to the Heavens, where the Heavenly Grandfather – who is also the immortal of all immortals and gods, the Jade Emperor – resided. After this announcement, Stone-Monkey scanned his surroundings with his super vision. As he did so, two beams of light shot out of his eyes, and the glare caught the Jade Emperor's attention. He sent two first-rank heavenly guards to see whose light this was.

"It looks like the light is coming from Huaguo Shan," said the first heavenly guard, General Ears-that-Follow-the-Wind.

"It is only a monkey," reported the second heavenly guard, whose name was General Eyes-that-See-a-Thousand-Miles. "When he eats and sleeps, the light disappears."

And so the Jade Emperor thought nothing more of the stone monkey.

Free to roam the country of Aolai, Stone-Monkey stepped foot here, there and everywhere. Soon, he found a group of monkeys he could play with, and he was happy. They scampered about and ate the many fruits that Huaguo Shan had to offer. Lychees, peaches and longans filled the monkeys' tummies, and edible flowers made healthy snacks. Dangling tree roots provided ropes for them to swing from tree to tree. At night, they huddled together in the crook of a branch and slept soundly under the moonlight. When the weather was hot and humid, they swam in the stream and sunbathed on its banks.

"Where does the water come from?" an inquisitive monkey asked. This made every monkey curious, especially Stone-Monkey.

"Whoever finds the source will be our king," declared the loudest monkey in the troop.

This inspired Stone-Monkey. He was determined to be the one to find the answer. So he swam upstream until he came to a curtain of water that seemed to be pouring down from high above. He had never seen anything like it, nor heard such a thundering noise – the roar of the water was deafening.

Unfazed by the strong downpour, he walked through the falling water and discovered a cave behind it.

Stone-Monkey returned to the rest of his troop and brought them to the source of the stream that he had discovered.

"I am now your king," Stone-Monkey announced as he stepped out from behind the water curtain. "And we shall make this cave our new home. I hereby name it Cave of the Water Curtain."

King Stone-Monkey and his troop continued to live a happy life, frolicking in the grassy hills, enjoying the delicious fruits and flowers, and sleeping when they were tired in the Cave of the Water Curtain.

Life was good for about three or four hundred years before King Stone-Monkey became melancholic.

"Oh, my king, what saddens you?" a spritely young monkey asked as he picked the fleas from his grandfather's coat.

"Nothing lasts for ever," Stone-Monkey replied, and, thinking out loud, he continued, "While I have had the good fortune to live for hundreds of years, one day I, too, will be gone – *poof!* Grabbed from this happiness by Yama, the God of Death and the Underworld."

"Ah, yes!" An older monkey sighed, shuddering at the thought. "Not long for me now, my king! There are only three types of beings that can escape death: buddhas, immortals and holy sages. All of them live in the ancient caves far, far away from here."

"Then I must find them," Stone-Monkey said. "To learn the secret of their longevity, and how I can live for ever."

His loyal troop prepared a farewell feast of sweet tangerines and peaches, juicy stalks of sugar cane, ruby-red pomegranates, and various flowers and small fruits. They even built him a raft so that he could follow the curve of the river to the ocean that would lead their king to other corners of the world.

"Thank you, my friends and subjects,"

Stone-Monkey said. Then, with a bound and a leap, he left his cave home and the mountain of his birth to sail for the southern continent.

After a long journey, he set foot on an island that was occupied by humans. Stone-Monkey looked for an immortal who could tell him the secret to eternal life, but, alas, the humans were no sages. So, after nearly ten years of searching, Stone-Monkey left on a new raft and sailed to the western continent.

When he saw the tip of a mountain peeking out from behind a cloud, he rowed his raft towards dry land and disembarked. There, he met a woodcutter who told him to go approximately eight miles south to the Tilted Moon and Three Stars Cave, in the Holy Wutai Mountain.

"There you'll find an immortal who will tell you the secret to eternal life," the woodcutter said before stalking off.

Indeed, when Stone-Monkey followed the woodcutter's instructions he reached the abode of Subodhi, an immortal who was known as the Patriarch of the West.

"Tell me, O Master Subodhi, the secret to longevity," Stone-Monkey beseeched.

"Where have you come from?" Subodhi asked, shocked that a mere monkey with a countenance of stone dared to ask for the secret to long life.

"I'm from Aolai, born on Huaguo Shan, and I made my home in the Cave of Water Curtain," said Stone-Monkey.

"Liar! Throw him out, disciples!" At this, Subodhi's congregation of thirty trainee immortals prepared to banish Stone-Monkey from their land.

"I'm not lying, Master Subodhi," said Stone-Monkey, desperately kowtowing before Subodhi. "I started my journey more than ten years ago and I've finally found you, an immortal."

"Halt!" Subodhi commanded his followers. "The monkey is not lying. It takes this length of time to cross the oceans to reach our land. This monkey has perseverance, which is essential for learning magic. What is your name?"

"Alas," Stone-Monkey replied, "I have no name and no parents, for I was born from a divine stone egg."

"Then I shall name you," Subodhi said.

"Oh, yes please, Master Subodhi. I would love a name to call myself."

"Your family name will be Sun, meaning *child*. And based on the rotation of given names, you are number ten in the cycle, so you'll be Wukong. Sun Wukong, the one who has awoken to nothing."

"Thank you, O Master Subodhi. Nothing can only be combated by doing something, and I swear to do so. I will make great progress. But first, teach me how I can be immortal."

"This would require that you learn the Tao, which would take many, many generations because there are three hundred and sixty schools of thought and actions in Taoism that lead to enlightenment."

"Will enlightenment bring immortality?" Sun Wukong was eager to know in his impatience to become immortal.

"Not at all, unless you learn the Seventy-two Transformations, in order to escape the Three Calamities, sent every five hundred years to punish those who seek immortality."

"Then that's not for me. I just want to live for ever and ever, and do nothing at all but bask in the sun and feed on fruits and flowers. Master, perhaps there are other ways I can have eternal life like this?"

Subodhi continued to list the different methods that would help Sun Wukong gain more wisdom, strength and energy, and to gain eternal life, but the monkey rejected them all. Exasperated, Subodhi whacked Sun Wukong three times on the head with the palm of his hand. Then he instructed his disciples to take Sun Wukong away and show him how to clean himself and learn the etiquette required to be a good student of Taoism.

"How rude of you!" a disciple said to Sun Wukong as Subodhi left with his hands behind his back and shut the door to his chambers behind him. "Subodhi has offered to teach you all the ways of the Tao and you've rejected them and offended him. Such an opportunity is hard to come by, I'll have you know. Who knows when the master will emerge from his room again?"

But Sun Wukong knew exactly what Subodhi was telling him by his symbolic message: three whacks on the head meant that the master was available on the third change of guard, which was when Sun Wukong should visit his chambers. And walking off with his hands behind his back meant that Sun Wukong was to enter the master's bedroom from the back door.

When night came, Sun Wukong followed a trail of fireflies to Subodhi's chambers, where he was welcomed by the immortal.

"Ah, you are indeed a child of Heaven and Earth,

of Yin and Yang," said Subodhi, "for only such a progeny would understand and be able to solve my riddle. Now, listen to me. There is no elixir to immortality. The Tao is a mysterious, magical force – a combination of female and male energies, of dark and light forces. It governs the skies and the earth, the animals and fish, the lakes and mountains. Not even gods and immortals are above the Tao. If this magic is shown to an imperfect being, then the master's words are nothing but fluff, and his mouth spews nonsense. But to the one who is ready to receive Taoism, every word the master says is like a stepping stone that leads the person to their destination."

"Master, I am all ears. I am hungry to learn the mysterious Tao. I didn't want to show the other disciples how eager I was, so I pretended to reject everything you'd offered to teach me. Please forgive me. Teach me the magic of the Tao." Sun Wukong knelt down and bowed his head until it touched the ground, respectfully thanking Subodhi.

"I know that you are, because I can tell that you're indeed a special monkey, even though you're also lazy and naughty. You can kowtow to me all you want, until your forehead is sore from touching the ground repeatedly, Sun Wukong. But all that kowtowing will amount to nothing if you don't understand that learning the Tao requires hard work and discipline, to control the mind," continued Subodhi.

"Master, I am willing to work hard and focus all my energies and strengths to learning everything that you have to teach me. I will learn to tame my mind, which I would admit does stray all over the place. I will learn to focus on the Tao."

Satisfied that Sun Wukong would put in the work to learning the Tao from him, Subodhi whispered wisdom into the monkey's ears for several minutes. In the magical Holy Wutai Mountain, the length of time is fluid for an immortal, and a thousand years can be condensed to a few years, a few minutes, a few seconds, all depending on how much of a hurry the immortal is in. After memorizing all that Subodhi had to tell him, Sun Wukong spent time in secret every day practising the exercises that would help preserve his life. Subodhi would appear every now and then to watch and tutor his favourite disciple.

Under Subodhi's tutoring, Sun Wukong learned cloud-somersaulting, which enabled him to travel so fast that Sun Wukong had travelled 108,000 miles and back before Subodhi had swallowed his next spoon of rice soup. Cloud-somersaulting can only be achieved through harnessing the power of the mind, xin. Sun Wukong also learned the magic of the Seventy-two Transformations, which enabled him to change form. This required Sun Wukong to understand how to transfer mind energies from one thing to another.

"Look at how magnificent I am. What the xin thinks, the being becomes, for I am what I think," Sun Wukong boasted to the other trainee immortals. Then he proceeded to change himself into a pine tree and back into his original form.

"Ahhh! See, it's really quite easy. By putting your mind to something, you can do anything." Sun Wukong chortled, metamorphosing again. "I don't understand how you have all been here for so long and still haven't learned how to change shapes."

Some of the trainee immortals gasped in wonder at the speed at which Sun Wukong had learned shapeshifting, while others felt the bitter bile of jealousy creeping up their throats. There were those who became angry at Sun Wukong, and they were the ones who complained the loudest to their master.

Subodhi's face reddened with anger when he heard of Sun Wukong's antics. "Sun Wukong! There is no room here for haughtiness or disrespect for the mysterious Tao. You are forever banished from Tilted Moon and Three Stars Cave. You must leave the Holy Wutai Mountain and never return."

"But, Master, what have I done wrong? I have perfected cloud-somersaulting and the Seventy-two Transformations like you've taught me. I listened to the words you whispered in my ears and memorized them diligently, and now I'm the best of your disciples. There's no being as perfect as me!"

"Leave! Now that the other disciples can see what you can do, you've made it very dangerous to stay here, for envy and jealousy are not good companions, and you've now endangered yourself since you lack the humility to keep the secrets of Taoism to yourself. If you do not change your ways and you continue to be so greedy, your hunger for immortality will be your downfall. Even eagerness has its limit, Sun Wukong."

"Please forgive me. I beg you, Master!"

But there was nothing that Sun Wukong could say or do to convince Subodhi to let him stay.

And so, after twenty years of learning the Tao, Sun Wukong returned to Huaguo Shan, heavy-hearted with regret at displeasing his master. He had learned a difficult lesson about greed, boastfulness and arrogance.

But this is not the end of the story of Sun Wukong. Very soon, he would leave the Cave of the Water Curtain again for another adventure. This time, he would find a size-changing staff, and in the future he would go on to battle the Bull-demon King, and later accompany Xuanzang the monk to India to bring the Buddhist sutra of Great Perfection of Wisdom to the Middle Kingdom.

Sun Wukong would go on one hundred adventures after leaving the Tilted Moon and Three Stars Cave. It is said that with each one, Sun Wukong became stronger – both in magical powers and in character. So much so that generations later he would gain the status of a god. Through the obstacles he overcame and the demons he slayed along the way, Sun Wukong became immortalized in the memories and imaginations of the people who heard of his adventures. And, with every triumph, he continued to learn that humility is the way to enlightenment, and immortality is not something you strive to achieve but something that is bestowed upon you only when you have earned it.

MR. MOLE FINDS A HUSBAND FOR HIS DAUGHTER

This is a cherished Korean folktale that is linked to the country's creation myth but also stands apart from it. The story is about a doting father who sets out to look for a worthy husband for his daughter, only to find that the best son-in-law is not very far away at all. Variants of tales involving a loving father seeking a husband for his daughter also exist in other parts of the world.

In the beginning, there was Mireuk and Seongka, who created the world alongside each other. Mireuk ruled humans with order and justice, while Seongka disturbed them with his mischievous antics, thus creating chaos and conflicts. Being one who hated sharing, it was Seongka who wanted to be the *only* god to rule the world. To do this, he challenged Mireuk to a competition. If he won, he would be the ruler of the world. But the God of Creation was not fazed – he was convinced he could not be beaten so easily by Seongka, who he considered an imposter. They agreed on three combats, and that winning all three would make one of them the supreme ruler of the world.

Mireuk won the first two: he froze a river solid in midsummer, and toppled Seongka in a tug of war at sea. Then it came to their third trial.

"I'll wager that you can't grow flowers from your body," Seongka said.

Tired from his triumphs, Mireuk said, "I bet you I can. But first we must each rest and harness our energy."

Mireuk was a kind and fair god. He wanted Seongka to rest as well before the next challenge, which would require both of them to channel their inner qi, the force that lies in all beings. Mireuk knew that one must be strong in the mind and body before qi could flow.

Mireuk sat cross-legged under a tree by the Kingin River and meditated for hours. He cleared his mind of other thoughts and focused his third eye on colourful and fragrant flowers. Then, when he finished meditating, he fell asleep under the moonlight. As he slept, flowers started to grow from the top of his head.

When Seongka saw this, he immediately stole the flowers.

"Mireuk is a cheat," Seongka lamented. "The flower creation should be done when we are awake, not asleep. And since nobody knows this except me, I will have everyone believe that the flowers grew from me instead."

With this, Seongka stuck the flowers on his own head and declared that *he* was the winner of this challenge.

When Mireuk woke from his slumber and discovered that Seongka had usurped him through trickery, the creator-god disappeared, never to be seen again. And this was how chaos, cunning and manipulation entered humankind.

To pray for the return of good and purity, the

people carved a likeness of Mireuk from a colossal rock and placed it near the spot where Mireuk had gone to sleep.

Many, many moons later, a family of moles came to live under the fertile ground where the statue of Mireuk stood. Abeoji Mole was a hard-working and devoted family man. His wife, Eomeoni Mole, was pious and prayed to Mireuk daily. She was kind of heart and pure in nature. The couple were delighted to know that they would soon be blessed with a child and their family would expand.

When Eomeoni Mole gave birth, it was to a daughter, and Abeoji Mole peered proudly at his offspring from behind his thick-rimmed glasses, his heart swelling with paternal pride.

"My daughter, your abeoji will always do his best by you, for this is a father's duty," he promised.

"Thank you, heaven above, for giving us a precious daughter to call our own," said Eomeoni Mole, praying at the feet of Mireuk's statue.

"Congratulations on the birth of your child, Eomeoni Mole," a small voice said as a black head peeked out from underneath Mireuk's left foot.

"Ah! Thank you, dear boy. You are so kind and polite," Eomeoni Mole said to their neighbour's young son, Mole-boy. "You are a good boy and not much older than our Mole-girl. When she's able to walk and talk, you must come over to play with her."

Mole-boy gladly agreed, then burrowed back underground to join his family.

When the Moles' daughter turned a hundred days old, a feast was prepared for guests who came from all over the forest to celebrate.

"Abeoji Mole, your role as her father is to find her the best husband, so she has the greatest chance of happiness when she is older," an elderly relative reminded Abeoji Mole during the festivity.

At once, Abeoji Mole set his mind on finding the best suitor to introduce to his precious Mole-girl. These thoughts preoccupied him throughout his daughter's childhood. Mole-girl grew to be an intelligent and loving child, spending time with her mother and father, learning about the world around them and playing happily with their neighbour, Mole-boy.

It seemed like no time at all until she had grown old enough to be married. Abeoji Mole hosted a meeting at his humble home, inviting all the elders from the mole clans around the country.

"Honourable elders, please offer your advice.

Who would make the best husband for my beautiful daughter?" Abeoji Mole asked.

"Ah, that would be Sky," replied an elder, raising his head to the Heavens.

"Hear, hear," the rest of the elders agreed. "Who could be greater?"

Abeoji Mole thanked everyone and immediately went to speak to Sky. "Sky, you reign from above in greatness and glory. You would make the perfect husband for my daughter. Would you like to meet her?"

"I assure you that I am not the greatest," Sky said in his cyan coat. "I can turn grey and thundery in a bad mood. You had better introduce your daughter to Sun, who is far more glorious than me."

"But why would you say this, Sky?" Abeoji Mole asked in surprise. "Every mole elder agreed that *you* are the greatest."

Sky disagreed. "Sun shines hot and bright. When he sleeps, the world is blanketed in darkness and the stars twinkle to greet him. When he wakes, flowers turn their faces towards his smile and birds chirp in delight to see the dimples on his cheeks. He, Abeoji Mole, is far more suited to be your son-in-law."

Hearing this, Abeoji Mole went in search of Sun.

"Your dazzling highness, you are warm, bright and a giver of life. You would make the perfect husband for my daughter. Would you like to meet her?" he asked.

"You are a wonderful baba, Abeoji Mole, but I'm afraid I cannot marry your daughter."

"But why, Sun?" asked Abeoji Mole. "You come highly recommended by Sky."

"Have you not noticed? When I'm angered, the grass scorches and the land cracks open. Rivers dry up and humans become parched and die. Your daughter will never be able to look me in the eye because I will blind her. Cloud is a far better match for her."

Thanking Sun, Abeoji Mole then went in search of Cloud. He finally found him curled up in a cumulus, all soft and fluffy. "Gentle Cloud, you quench the thirst of the land below, allowing life to thrive. You would make the perfect husband for my daughter. Would you like to meet her?" he asked.

"Me?" said Cloud, his cheeks puffing into a smile. "You don't want me for your son-in-law, Abeoji Mole."

"But why not? Sun says you'll be the best bridegroom for my daughter."

"Let me show you why," said Cloud. He sucked the air into his mouth until his cheeks swelled and his face turned stormy. He let out his breath and a terrible storm tore through the sky. Rain fell in torrents, flooding the fields. Thunder rumbled. Bolts of lightning crackled.

"So do you see why it's best I am not your daughter's husband? Wind would be a far better son-in-law than me. He will sweep your daughter off her feet."

Determined to find the best suitor for his child, Abeoji Mole thanked Cloud and went in search of Wind. Shielding his face from the debris blowing about him, Abeoji Mole said, "Wind, you are powerful and strong. You would make the perfect husband for my daughter. Would you like to meet her?"

The grass stopped rustling and the leaves stood still as Wind replied, "I may be strong, Abeoji Mole, but nothing is as strong as stone. See the statue of Mireuk? No matter how hard I whip him, he is unperturbed. No matter how loudly I roar, he is untroubled. Even when I softly tickle him with a light breeze, he remains straight-faced. Now, that is determination. He will surely make the greatest husband for your daughter."

Weary and forlorn at his failure, Abeoji Mole

dragged his feet home. When he came to the statue of Mireuk, he bowed before it and told the statue of his woes. The statue listened and, with great compassion, he parted his thick stone lips and said, "Abeoji Mole, I see how hard you've searched for a worthy husband for your daughter. Your determination has not gone unnoticed and neither has your abundant love for your precious child. But I am not the one for her."

"Oh, great Mireuk, then who is?" asked Abeoji Mole.

"There is one very like you – determined, industrious and generous. His heart is golden and his thoughts flow pure like clearest water. With his spade-like hands, he shovels earth from the base of my feet to make a home for his family, and one day he shall surely topple me if he keeps digging deep. He is ready for a wife, Abeoji Mole, and if you only look, you will see that he already makes your daughter very happy."

"What? Who? Where?" Abeoji Mole asked in great excitement. "Lead me to this most suitable candidate for he sounds just like the kind of husband for my daughter that I've been searching the whole world for."

"There he is, Abeoji Mole. Your neighbour's son,

Mole-boy, from your own community. He will make the perfect husband for your wonderful daughter."

"Oh, hello, Abeoji Mole! Have you had your breakfast?" Mole-boy asked politely, just as his mother had taught him to – because it is always good manners to ask if an elderly person has filled their tummy.

Abeoji Mole wasted no time in asking Mole-boy if he would like to marry his daughter. And because Mole-boy had been in love with Abeoji Mole's daughter since he was young, and she with him, he could only say yes. Right away, Mole-boy proposed, and Mole-girl accepted with great delight.

This ends the story of how Mireuk the creator-god still channelled goodness and purity to the world, even in the form of a statue, leading Abeoji Mole and his daughter to happiness. After this, there was much rejoicing at the feet of Mireuk as all the moles in the forest came to celebrate the joining of two great families. It goes without saying that the mole couple lived happily ever after.

CRAB AND MONKEY GO TO WAR

This age-old Japanese folktale about friendship gone wrong is said to explain the reason why monkeys and crabs do not get along. Like many ancient stories, it also uses both animals and physical objects to show how people can sometimes behave – including in times of cruelty and revenge. While modern readers may find some of the events of the tale upsetting, it is a very famous and important piece of documented Japanese folktale, and therefore historic. It has been translated into English by several European translators, and Yei Evelyn Theodora Kate Ozaki included it in her 1908 book, Japanese Fairytales. *Variants of the tale exist all over Japan, and this is another retelling.*

Early one morning, a monkey and a crab each went out for a walk. Although they set out at different times and at different speeds, it was not long later that they met at the curve of the mountainous road.

"Oh, hello, Crab!" said Monkey.

"Why, good morning, Monkey!" Crab greeted Monkey in return.

After these pleasantries, Monkey spied the rice ball that Crab held in one of her pincers.

"Ah, an onigiri, Crab! That was a lucky find," Monkey said, his mouth watering, for he loved nothing more than a nice toasted rice ball as a snack.

"Yes, Monkey! Today is my lucky day," Crab replied, impatient to get on her way and finish eating her delicious onigiri.

"See here, Crab? I have a persimmon seed, which is much better than your rice ball." Monkey rummaged in the fur of his chest, where he had hidden the seed.

"A persimmon seed? What would I do with it?" Crab asked, making tracks to leave.

"Wait, my friend! Surely you can see that a seed is worth more than one rice ball? Just think about what you can do with all the persimmons this little seed will bring forth."

Now, although Crab was reluctant to part with

her rice ball, she considered the long-term benefits of planting a persimmon seed. She thought of her children and grandchildren, who would be able to enjoy the succulent fruit when they were in season. She thought of her neighbours and friends, who would also delight in the tree's sweet and delicious bounty. With these happy thoughts, Crab handed her rice ball to Monkey.

"Thank you, most gracious Crab!" he said. "Here's your seed."

"My pleasure, most honourable Monkey! You're a good friend indeed."

When Crab returned home, she planted the black persimmon seed, and before long a tree grew from the spot where it had been sown. And soon after that, orange persimmons hung from its branches.

"But how do I get up the tree to enjoy those fruits?" Crab despaired.

Just then, Monkey walked by and saw the delicious persimmons. He scampered up the tree and started to eat the juicy fruit, one by one.

"Monkey, Monkey, do you remember me?" Crab shouted, waving her claw. She recognized Monkey from the ring of white fur on his chest where he had tucked his persimmon seed.

"Crab, is that you? Your rice ball was most delicious, by the way!"

"I'm glad you enjoyed my rice ball. As you can see, your seed has borne fruit, but I can't get to them. I should've realized that crabs can't climb trees. Silly me! Would you be so kind as to pick some juicy persimmons for me, Monkey?"

"Oh yes, you *should've* realized that you can't climb, Crab! What were you thinking?" Monkey laughed at Crab.

As Monkey was feeling extremely cheeky that day, he decided to play a trick on Crab. He picked a succulent persimmon and gobbled that up. With his other hand, he plucked an unripe one and threw it at Crab.

"Hey, that's not ripe. It's too hard to eat! Come on, be a good sport and throw me down a soft and juicy one."

Monkey picked another persimmon, and this time he aimed it at Crab's head.

"Ouch!" Crab cried, rubbing her sore head.

Monkey thought it funny and did it again. *Plonk!*

"Ow! Stop it, Monkey!" Crab said as a hairline crack began to appear in her shell.

But Monkey simply laughed once more. It seemed that he was not aware it is terrible to laugh at other people's suffering and misfortune.

Down rained more unripe persimmons – so hard that when they hit the ground they bounced about like tennis balls. Crab hopped to the left and she hopped to the right, trying her best to avoid being hit. Monkey could not stop chuckling at the hilarity of Crab's dance! He laughed until tears rolled down his face.

"Monkey, you will surely be punished by Heaven and Earth for your bad behaviour!" Crab said as she dodged more bouncing persimmons.

"Never! I'm only having a bit of fun, Crab!" Monkey replied as he continued to throw unripe persimmons at her. "The Heavenly and Earthly gods do not punish those who are only having a laugh; they punish those who are mean! I challenge them to punish me if I'm being mean today."

A loud *CRACK* made Monkey stop his antics. Another rock-hard persimmon had fallen on Crab's head and her shell was now split wide open. Holding her head with her claws, Crab quickly scurried back home to her family.

"Okaasan, what happened?" her children asked as they hurried to help their mother to her bed.

Crab proceeded to tell her family about Monkey's cruel antics as the eldest of her children bandaged her mother's head. The second of her children boiled herbal broths to feed her mother. The third of Crab's children massaged her mother's sore head to make her feel better. For days, everyone did their best to make Crab feel comfortable. But, alas, there was nothing her children and grandchildren could do to mend her cracked shell. It was an injury that could not be survived. Very soon, poor Crab withered away.

"This is simply not fair," one of Crab's children cried. "Our mother did nothing but good. She did not deserve this. All Monkey had to do was pick some ripe persimmons for her, and instead he did this. He is indeed a very cruel monkey."

"She sacrificed her rice ball for a seed and this was her end," another one of Crab's children said. "We must avenge her death. A lesson must be taught."

"Let us gather some friends we can trust and find a way to get back at Monkey," the last of her children said. "We must show the monkeys of the world that this is no way to behave, especially to your friends."

And so the crab children set out to find allies for their mission.

They left their home and went from village to village telling their mother's story. They carried a banner that said "Friends of Crab Club". This attracted the attention of a pile of dung, which said that it would help. A bumblebee buzzed by and read the banner and asked a few questions. Bumblebee was aghast at how awfully Monkey had behaved and immediately signed up to join the club. The troop moved on and soon came to another village.

There they gathered in the square and the eldest of Crab's children started to sing a plaintive song about her mother's story. An usu rolled by and volunteered his service.

"I'm sure you could use the help of a mortar, for this is what I am," barrel-like Usu said, pounding his chest to show his strength, "I will not be a bystander. I will be an upstander, standing up for Crab and others." The three crab children welcomed Usu as an ally.

The next morning, Dung, Bumblebee, Usu and the crabs returned to the persimmon tree, where they knew they would find Monkey. He now had an orange stain around his mouth and on his cheeks from stuffing his face with persimmons.

"Monkey, throw us some of those delicious persimmons," Usu said.

"No way, you batter-head!" Monkey replied,

bounding higher up the tree for more fruit.

Usu used all his might to roll into the trunk of the persimmon tree, thumping it hard. A muffled "Hey, stop!" came from Monkey as he gobbled up the last bite of his persimmon. Usu ignored Monkey and carried on bashing the trunk the way he would be used for pummelling rice grains into flour.

Bam! Bam! Bam!

The tree was shaking so hard that Monkey found himself hanging on for dear life as he dangled from a branch.

"Hey, Usu! Stop it!" Monkey said. And before he could say anything more, Monkey found himself falling, and he plopped down hard on Dung.

"Oh, poo-ey!" Monkey cried as he had a whiff of Dung. "Look what you made me do, Usu!"

Monkey tried to detach himself from the sticky heap, but Dung kept making Monkey skid and fall. Up Monkey got again, and down Monkey slid once more as Dung clung to Monkey's legs and feet. Soon Monkey was face down in Dung, spluttering, with his bottom in the air.

Bzz! Bzz! Bzz! Bumblebee buzzed towards Monkey, making a beeline for his buttocks. She stung him right there, where it hurt the most.

"OUCH!" Monkey cried as he rubbed his sore bottom, his face covered in dung. And just when Monkey thought he'd had enough bad luck, Crab's children and grandchildren gathered around the naughty creature, snapping their claws.

Sounds of *clip, clip, clip* were followed by a series of *ow, ow, ow,* echoing throughout the town, as Crab's kin snipped the hairs off Monkey's bottom with their razor-sharp claws.

Crab's neighbours and friends cheered and clapped in glee. They would not usually find entertainment in the misery of others, but they felt Monkey deserved to be punished for how he'd treated the innocent Crab. He got his comeuppance for being cruel after all – and not by the gods of Heaven or Earth but by a troop of loyal allies and kinfolk.

THE NOT-SO-VERY-CLEVER WOLF

In Mongolia, the tradition of oral storytelling is as ancient as the land itself. Stories told in tents have been passed down by word of mouth from mother to daughter, father to son, generation to generation. They mirror the nomadic life of the Mongolians, many of whom continue to live in the Great Steppe like their ancestors, where the land is sprawling, life is wild and the weather is harsh. Not every story has a serious lesson to teach; many are shared because they are fun to tell. In this Mongolian folktale, a silly wolf suffers the consequences of his foolish ways.

Once upon a time, a wolf went for a walk in the Great Steppe of Mongolia. The sun was bright, and the billowing clouds that covered the blue sky above changed shapes as the wind blew across the expanse of land. It ruffled up Wolf's black-grey coat as his stomach rumbled in hunger. It had been days since he had eaten a good meal. He went on prowling, looking for something to fill his tummy, when he came across a blood-sausage lying on the ground.

Delighted, he pawed at the sausage, rolling it around on the ground where feather grass called stipa grew in bunches. He sniffed the sausage with his narrow snout. "Oh, you do smell delicious!" Wolf said.

He opened his mouth wide and was about to take a bite when a voice said, "Mister Wolf, do not eat me, I beseech you!"

"Who speaks?" Wolf asked, looking around. "Is it you, Stipa?"

"Not me," the feather grass replied.

Wolf opened his jaw wide and was about to take a bite of the blood-sausage when the same voice said, "Mister Wolf, do not eat me, I beg you!"

"Who speaks?" Wolf asked again rather foolishly, his head turning left and right. "Is it you, Savannah?"

"Not us," the shrubs and grasses replied.

Very hungry now, Wolf wanted nothing but to gobble up the blood-sausage – so much so that saliva dripped from his fangs. Curling his lips to take a chomp, he heard the same voice say once more, "Mister Wolf, please do not eat me!"

"Who speaks?" Wolf asked, bewildered that it was proving so difficult to eat something right under his very nose.

"It is I, the blood-sausage," said the voice.

"Why can't I eat you when you're just lying there for all the animals of the steppes to devour?"

"Mister Wolf, not far from here is a Mongolian wild horse, a mare, and she has got stuck in the mud. To eat her for breakfast would be a much greater privilege, for her meat is most delicious."

"How far do I have to walk to get to this horse?" asked Wolf.

"Ah, only about one hundred steps, and if you run, Mister Wolf, it would take you fifty strides and half the time to get to this mare," said the sausage.

Wolf, who really had no sense of time and numbers, agreed that a whole fresh horse was better than a small dried-up sausage, and decided to run with the wind towards the wild mare.

By the time Wolf arrived at his destination, it was almost midday and the sun was blazing hot above him. His tongue hung out of his mouth as he panted, looking for water, but there were only mud pools to be found. Soon, Wolf came to a mud pool where, sure enough, a horse stood helplessly, stuck in the mud up to her knees. She must have been there for hours, for her back was burnt, bronzed by the glaring savannah sun. An eagle circled overhead as the horse's mane and tail whipped hard to chase away the buzzing flies.

Forgetting that he was thirsty and seeing that the mare could not run away, Wolf opened his mouth to take a bite of her rump.

"Wait! What are you doing, Wolf?" she cried.

"A blood-sausage told me that a wild horse is much more delicious than a silly sausage. So I am here to eat you, Horse!"

"Can't you see that I am not a horse? You are the silly sausage yourself!"

"Not a horse?" said Wolf. "Then what are you?"

"I am an ass!" replied the Mongolian wild ass, which was known as a khulan.

"Ah! You must taste better than a horse, I suppose. Donkeys, I've been told, are flavourful and gamey, with meat fit for emperors. But wait… Is an ass the same as a donkey?"

"Well, Wolf, all you need to know is that all asses are donkeys and all donkeys are horses. You can call us cousins if you like."

Wolf looked at Khulan and the wild ass detected a flash of bewilderment in his eyes.

"Never mind what I am," she said. "To eat me, you need to unstick me."

Wolf scratched his head in confusion. "Ah! What do I do?"

"You have to pull me out, of course! See that outcrop over there? It's where Steppe Eagle has her nest. In there, you will find a rope, which you can tie round my neck and pull me out with."

And so Wolf padded towards Steppe Eagle's nest. In the flat nest were eaglets that chirped, waiting for their mother to drop food into their mouths.

"Don't eat us, Wolf," an eaglet pealed. "Our mother will peck your eyes out with her sharp beak."

"Oh, I'm not here to eat you, eaglets," replied Wolf. "I am here to look for a rope. Khulan said that there is a rope in your nest."

The eaglets giggled at Wolf's words. They were amused that Wolf did not know that eagles do not make ropes. One of the eaglets screeched, "Wolf, we don't have a rope. You'd best go back to Khulan to let her know."

Off Wolf went back to the mud pool to find that Khulan had just managed to get herself out of the mud. Meanwhile, he was getting more and more hungry.

"Ah, Wolf, you're back! I have a message for you from Steppe Eagle, who saw you prowling at her nest. She flies above us keeping watch. Luckily for you, she didn't attack you with her talons and hooked mouth when she saw you near her babies."

"What was the message?" Wolf sighed, now feeling less and less energetic.

"It's on the hoof of my left hind leg," said Khulan.

And so Wolf circled Khulan to find the best spot from which to read the message from Steppe Eagle. Just as he reached her left back hoof, she kicked out and walloped Wolf hard with both hind legs! He went flying and landed on a pile of dried feather grass.

"Ee-haw! Silly Wolf!" brayed Khulan. "Why would Steppe Eagle leave a message on my hoof?"

Wolf lay dazed, having been tricked and outwitted by all the food that could have been his dinner.

In fact, soon after, the not-so-very-clever wolf was caught by a family of nomads who were hunting for fur for the upcoming winter, so he never got his meal.

This playful, subversive story of traditionally weaker prey outsmarting a typically cunning predator can be read as a reminder to commit to one's decisions without faltering. The foolish wolf should have eaten that sausage while he had the chance, but instead he was easily led on a merry chase by those who were sharper-minded than him.

TALES OF THE GOOD, WISE AND BRAVE

This trio of stories is about ordinary people doing and encountering extraordinary things – a boy born from a peach, who went on to fight the king of demons; a young girl who disguised herself as a man so her ageing father would not have to go to war; and a young boy whose story of intelligence and selflessness has been used to teach Chinese children about good character and meaningful deeds for centuries. These folktales have endured the passing of time, retold through the generations in books and films. These legendary heroes and heroines are immortalized in their nation's history and the people's imaginations.

KONG RONG AND THE PEAR

Kong Rong was born in the year 153 in the state of Lu in northern China, during the Eastern Han dynasty (25–220 BCE). He was a renowned Chinese poet, politician and military leader, and this story of the fraternal love and respect shown by Kong Rong to his brothers is mentioned in the Three Character Classic, *or* San Zi Jing – *a thirteenth-century classic text that was used to educate Chinese children from the Song dynasty (960 to 1279) until the late 1800s of the Qing dynasty (1644 to 1912) on good character and the importance of meaningful action. The* Three Character Classic *text is said to be written by two Song dynasty authors, Wang Yinglin and Ou Shizi.*

This retelling gives us a peek into what the kind, loving and generous four-year-old Kong Rong was like, and points to the reasons for his later success.

It was a blistering hot day in the state of Lu, in the town in which Kong Rong lived. The air was still, and the fields beyond the house were parched, with patches of brown in many places.

At that moment, Kong Rong's father, Kong Zhou, was away. Kong Zhou was a captain tasked with keeping Mount Tai, a sacred mountain not far from the family home, safe from invasion. Every year, Kong Zhou protected the emperor of the state of Lu when he journeyed to Mount Tai on his annual pilgrimage to give thanks to Heaven and Earth for granting him the celestial permission to rule China.

Kong Zhou ran a tight ship in the family home – he was strict, but he was also a loving and fair father. While he was away, Kong Rong and his six brothers remained indoors to escape the beating summer sun, dutifully reading and studying in the family hall, as they knew would please their father.

Kong Rong was practising his writing, learning the strokes to write the Chinese character for the word *pear*, lí (梨). This was the homework that his father had set for him before he went on his royal mission. It was not an easy feat for a four-year-old to write even the simplest of Chinese characters, let alone one with this many strokes, and Kong Rong was grumpy.

Being the sixth son, he was fortunate to have five older brothers he could learn from.

"How will I ever get this right?" said Kong Rong sulkily, his arms folded across his chest.

"There are a lot of strokes, I agree," said Kong Rong's eldest brother patiently, looking up from his book. "Here, let me show you how."

He held Kong Rong's hand in his as he guided the four-year-old boy, helping him to write with a fine calligraphy brush. Afterwards, Kong Rong made lines and dots, copying his eldest brother as best as he could.

"Thank you, Da Ge," said Kong Rong, calling him by his title, meaning Elder Brother.

"Practice makes perfect," said Kong Rong's second big brother lovingly. "Start from the top and don't press your brush down too hard, or the ink will blot and make a smudge on the paper. See, like this."

Kong Rong did as he was shown by his second big brother and, indeed, he found that a light feathery touch of the brush did not cause blotting and made his writing look much better.

One by one, his older brothers showed Kong Rong how to correctly write the Chinese character for lí, one stroke at a time.

All seven brothers got along very well, as their parents had taught them and expected of them. Their paternal ancestor, Confucius, had put together a book called the *Analects* that contained instructions on how to behave in the family.

According to Confucius, being a good and dutiful child involved more than being respectful and obedient. He said that children should be willing to make sacrifices for their parents' health and happiness. Many people still believe that when parents pass away, they become like gods who can bless the living, so they need to be honoured and revered.

Every year, the brothers and their parents would perform the ritual of Qing Ming, sweeping the ancestral tomb on the fifteenth day of spring. During this time, Cook would prepare special savoury and sweet sticky-rice dumplings, qingtuan. These would be packed in lacquer boxes and taken to the family ancestral tomb to be offered to the deceased, and to be shared with their extended family, who gathered at the tomb for this special occasion.

Kong Rong loved Qing Ming as he got to travel on horseback with his baba to the family's ancestral burial ground. He loved to light joss sticks for his ancestors and to help his baba, mama, aunts and uncles sweep and clean the family tomb. Plus, he was always excited to eat Cook's sweet qingtuan filled with mung-bean paste, while Elder Brother preferred the savoury ones, filled with pickled radish and bamboo shoots.

As well as the relationship between children and parents, Confucius had written about the love between brothers. He said that younger brothers should show the highest respect to their older brothers, with the most respect given to the eldest. Kong Rong's father had taught him this as soon as he could speak. When the youngest of the seven sons started to talk, this was what he was taught too. Kong Rong was always greeted by his title – Liu Ge, or Elder Sixth Brother – by his little brother, the baby in the family.

"I can't wait for Baba to come home," said Kong Rong's younger brother. He was playing with wooden blocks, building towers and walls with them. "I want to show Baba this long wall I've made. Look, Liu Ge."

"That is a great wall, Youngest Brother," said Kong Rong.

"You'll have to be patient, Youngest Brother. Baba will not be back for a few more weeks. The journey to Mount Tai is a long one, and Baba may be tired when he returns, so we must allow him to rest first," Elder Brother reminded him.

It was late in the afternoon several weeks later when Kong Zhou returned home. The sun was low in the sky, but the seven brothers were still reading and studying when their father strode into the family hall.

"My sons, my heart swells with pride to see you obeying orders," said Kong Zhou.

"Baba!" said all seven brothers in unison. They were excited to see their father after so many weeks of missing him.

"I have brought you a treat, as I promised," said Kong Zhou, waving a cloth sack in the air.

"What do you have, Baba?" asked the youngest of his sons, fidgeting with excitement.

"I have pears!" replied Kong Zhou, tousling the boy's hair. "These juicy and crunchy lí are just the right fruit for summer."

Kong Zhou tipped the cloth sack upside down, and seven golden pears of various sizes tumbled out.

He picked the biggest pear and offered it to his sixth son. "Kong Rong, since you've been learning to write the word lí for some time, you get to have the biggest pear," he said.

But, to Kong Zhou's surprise, Kong Rong shook

his head. "No, Baba, I don't deserve the biggest pear. I'd like the smallest one, please."

"Oh?" said Kong Zhou. "I'm very curious to know why you'd like the smallest pear."

"I'm younger than my five brothers above me, so Elder Brother should have the biggest pear," replied Kong Rong seriously.

"Ah!" said Kong Zhou. "But, by this logic, what would be the size of pear for your younger brother, the last of my sons?"

"I am older than him, so I feel I should also leave him a bigger pear than mine," replied Kong Rong, as seriously as before.

"Oh?" said Kong Zhou again. "My sixth son, you must explain this thinking to me, for I'm at a loss for words."

Kong Rong stepped forward and bowed before his father, showing him the respect that was expected.

"I love my brothers equally, Baba, and I want them to have a bigger pear than me," replied Kong Rong, even more seriously. "Taking the biggest pear for myself would give me no joy. Having my baby brother give me the biggest pear would also make me unhappy. So I would happily take the smallest. And because my brothers know that I've offered the biggest of the pears to them out of love, they are happy, which makes me happy."

"That is very kind and generous reasoning, Kong Rong," Kong Zhou said. "But there are seven pears of different sizes. By your logic, does it mean that Elder Brother should get the biggest, Second Brother the second biggest, and so on and so forth?"

"Indeed, Baba, because a person deserves the portions that are according to their rank. This is only fair. Wasn't this what Master Confucius taught us?" Kong Rong replied, after pausing to think.

"My son, your diplomacy will make you a great politician one day. A man of the state should always put the people's welfare before his own, as Master Confucius advised," said Kong Zhou, patting his son on the head. "And your diligence will make you a great scholar, someone who will continue in their education and contribute to the literature of our times."

"Thank you, Baba," replied Kong Rong. "Shall we share the pears now, as Youngest Brother has been eagerly waiting for his treat?"

And so that evening, in the state of Lu, seven brothers ate the pears that their father had brought home for them as a treat. Kong Rong had the smallest one, and he was the happiest one of them all.

HUA MULAN, THE MAIDEN WARRIOR

The story of Mulan, the maiden warrior, has to be the most widely recognizable legend from China. The story comes from an old folk song, known as the Ballad of Mulan, or Mulan Shi in Mandarin Chinese. Historians believe it was written during the Northern Wei dynasty, a turbulent time in Chinese history, which lasted from the fourth to the sixth centuries (386 to 535). The founders of this dynasty were the Tuoba, a nomadic tribe of people with Turkic ancestry, who fought to unite the northern self-ruling states under one emperor they called the Khan.

As time went by, the Ballad of Mulan *was sung so much that in the twelfth century a written copy was added to the* Yuefu Shiji, *a compiled anthology of folk poems. In this way, it was documented for posterity. Whether Mulan the maiden warrior was real or not, she is an unforgettable figure whose story has been retold through the ages in books and films, from China to Hollywood. This is a retelling, adapted from several sources.*

The night was about to turn into dawn. Hua Mulan galloped through the grasslands on the bare back of her chestnut mare, her black hair streaming behind her in the early-morning breeze.

"Nooooo!" Mulan shouted into the wind. "The world is my oyster. I will not marry the man who was chosen for me."

Mulan slowed her horse to catch her breath, her heart pounding against her rib cage so hard that her chest hurt. Sweat beaded on her brow and upper lip, and she burst into tears.

Her father, Hua Hu, was a commander of the Great Khan's army. He had sent word home from Black Mountain, three days' journey away, that she would soon be married to the prominent and eligible Wang Qingyun, the son of Wang Sixun. In marrying his daughter off to an elite Chinese family, Hua Hu was following in the tradition of his Turkic ancestors, the ancient nomadic Tuoba people who'd lived on the northern steppes between Mongolia and China for more than four hundred years.

"Daughter, you must behave more like a lady," Mulan's mother had pleaded when she'd learned the news. "You must now put away your coarse nomadic ways. Forget that you know martial arts, archery and horse riding. You will have no need for such abilities at the Wang household. There you'll be expected to use the wifely and feminine skills of weaving, embroidery and cooking, and later child-rearing. A marriage is a joining of two families, daughter, and you will represent your father's ancestors in the Wang household."

Mulan shuddered at these expectations, for this was not how she had envisioned her life to be. She knew she would be expected to get married one day, according to her father's heritage and customs. But she did not want to be married into a family such as the Wangs. They were of pure Han Chinese ancestry, unlike her, and their ways would be different to hers. Mulan's mother was Han Chinese, but she was no elite, and Hua Hu was no Tuoba royalty. Seventeen-year-old Mulan and her siblings, nine-year-old sister Manan and five-year-old brother Yaoer, had been raised in the nomadic way. Mulan was used to roaming freely on the steppe land surrounding the family's qionglu, a large tent made from felt. She was an excellent archer, and she helped her father hunt animals for meat and fur.

Meanwhile, her future husband was exempted from the army because he was a scholar, which would be attractive prospects in a husband for every other girl in China, but not for Mulan. She did not wish to be a scholar's wife, prevented from learning herself and expected to serve her husband, in accordance with Chinese customs. She wanted to be like her mother, who was regarded by her husband as his equal. Her parents' marriage was unique, formed out of choice, love and respect.

Being married to a scholarly Chinese family would put a stop to all the freedom she knew, and Mulan's heart ached with this knowledge. She was proud of her dual heritage, but she wanted to continue living the way she'd been brought up by her father – on the steppe with her horse, Mudan.

"You're a good girl, Mudan," Mulan whispered as she stroked the mare's chestnut mane. "What would I do without you?" She leaned against Mudan's neck and hugged her, nuzzling into her mane.

Just then, not far ahead in the grasslands, two chestnut hares bounded by.

"Ah! They will make a good stew for our dinner," Mulan said, pulling out her bow and an arrow from the quiver slung across her chest.

She aimed the arrow at the hares, who had stopped to nibble at some grass. When a rustle caused the hares to scamper off, Mulan lowered her bow and gave chase. Then, as the hares stopped bounding, coming to a rest side by side, Mulan aimed once more – and her swift arrow found both creatures in one stroke. Climbing down from Mudan, she picked up the animals and slung them over the mare's back.

"Mother will be pleased that we have meat, and Father will be proud that I aimed well, killing two hares with a single arrow," Mulan said. "Thank you, Heavens, for this generous find. We will have new skins for the coming winter, and a lovely meal tonight."

For a moment, Mulan forgot that she would soon be married. She quickly rode home on Mudan as the sun rose in the sky.

As Mulan entered her family's felt tent, she held both hares up. "Mother, look what I've caught. I wasn't planning on—" She froze mid-sentence.

Her mother was kneeling at the altar of Od Ana, the Goddess of Fire, with her face cupped in her hands, sobbing and praying for mercy.

"Mother, what has happened?" Mulan asked, dropping the hares to run to her mother's side.

"Your father is just back from Black Mountain. He said that the Khan is drafting again for a new army, and he needs to go to battle once more," Mulan's mother said, looking up at her daughter. "I'm afraid that he won't survive this one, given his age and health."

Mulan felt a stab of anguish in her heart. It was true – her father was surely not young and fit enough to endure another battle, and yet he had a duty to the Khan and could not refuse. The only way he could be spared was if there was a boy of fighting age in their family who could take his place. Mulan knew what she had to do.

"I will go in Father's place," Mulan said, wiping tears from her mother's face. "Yaoer is too young and I have no elder brother. The Khan's army will have to take me."

"But, Daughter, no girl has ever been conscripted before. This isn't possible!" Mulan's mother said in despair.

"I look enough like a boy, Mother," Mulan said, indicating her toned body and lean frame. "I will cut my hair short, and nobody will be able to tell that I'm a girl once I put on Father's armour. I'm better than any man on horseback, and my archery skills are the best in the steppe."

"Mudan is not a horse for battle," Mulan's mother

said, cupping her daughter's face in her hands. Looking intently into her eyes, she continued, "You may be the best archer on this side of the steppe, but the enemies have far more experience. I can't let you do this, Daughter."

"Mother, we have no choice! Father cannot go to battle. Don't worry. I will get a steed at the market east of here, and a saddle and blanket at the one west of us. I will need a bridle, and a long whip too. What I can't find at the east and west markets, I will get at the south and north ones. Please keep Mudan safe for me. Tell her I'll be back to ride her again," Mulan said, trying to stop her voice from breaking.

The next morning, as her sister and brother were still asleep, and their father's soft snores filled their tent, Mulan crept out of their qionglu, wearing her father's armour, with a roll of bedding and a sack of gold coins. Her mother bundled some air-dried meat into a felt sack and filled a sheep-stomach pouch with hot fermented milk tea, then slipped the food and drink into Mulan's satchel.

"Farewell, Daughter!" Mulan's mother whispered. "May your journey be smooth and blessed."

Mulan headed eastward, where she bought a steed

from the horse merchant in the market there. Then she rode the steed to purchase a saddle, a blanket and the rest of the things she needed. By the time she was done, the sun was nearly setting.

Pleased that she was fully equipped to join the Khan's army, Mulan rolled out her bedding and made a fire so she could camp under the stars for the night. But as she lay down to sleep, she realized that she had forgotten about her hair. Sitting back up, she took her hunting knife out from her satchel, and with the moon and bonfire as her light, she cut off her tresses until her hair was so short it stuck out in tufts from her head. She watched as the fire crackled, burning the bunches of hair she fed to it.

"Now I look like any young man joining the Great Khan's army," Mulan said, satisfied, as she swept her hands over her head.

She awoke at the crack of dawn, then put on her father's armour and rode towards the Yellow River. Determined to ride without wavering or distraction, she reached the river before sunset, camped there for the evening, and then made her way onwards to Black Mountain at the break of dawn the next day.

When she finally arrived, she saw a line of men queuing for conscription. She joined the line and found that they were being tested for their archery skills. Their target was a piece of hide stretched tightly over a wooden frame, painted with a small red circle in the centre.

When it came to Mulan's turn, she whipped an arrow from her quiver, aimed it confidently at the target – and hit the bullseye. Mulan was the only soldier to do so, and she was recruited into the army without hesitation. The Khan's commanders cheered and praised her for her masculine strengths and accuracy.

"Great shot, soldier! That target was a long distance away. Your eyesight is sharp," the captain of the Khan's archery battalion said. "Your name and status?"

"I am Hua Mulan, the first-born child of Hua Hu of the Tuoba clan. My father is aged and war-weary, and he has sent me in his place to fight for the Great Khan," Mulan said, making her voice a little low and gruff.

"You are a good son, Hua Mulan, and the God of War will grant your father permission to abstain from war. Your face is yet to grow hair, and we need young and able men like you to fight for the Khan's army. As the Great Khan's highest commanding officer here, I grant you permission to take your father's place at war," the captain said. "Here is a metal helmet to show that you are part of the Great Khan's army."

Mulan was sent into battle immediately, and she fought her first combat with fervour and focus. One year turned into two, and two into three, and soon time slipped away. As the years in battle passed, Mulan's combat skills developed. She learned to brandish the sword and to throw the vaulting pole, and excelled in using both. She even found a way to make her chain armour stronger to protect herself.

As soldier after soldier fell in combat, Mulan was able to stay alive. Before long, she rose in rank from a common soldier to a commanding officer. Mulan fought alongside men in battle for the Great Khan's army for twelve summers and winters. During that time, she crossed ten thousand miles of mountain passes and terrain, riding authoritatively on her steed. She protected her horse and herself from injury, until it was time for her horse to retire from battle due to old age.

Her prowess as an archer did not go unnoticed either, as her swift arrows flew past the heads of many soldiers to hit every target she aimed at. Mulan was rewarded again and again by the Great Khan himself. And when the war was over, he offered to promote her as a high-ranking official to lead his army.

"What is your heart's desire?" the Great Khan asked. "Your wish is my command."

"I've no need to be a high-ranking commander, my khan," Mulan replied. "All I ask for is a swift steed to ride back home to my family. After twelve years in combat, I've missed them, and they me. I would like to ask permission to retire from battle as my parents are ageing and I will need to take care of them."

The Khan nodded. "Indeed, as the first-born son, your filial duty is to your parents. I will send you home with a troop of guards, for a brave and mighty warrior like you requires a hero's send-off. I wish you well, Hua Mulan!"

Mulan was given the fastest horse in the army and, together with her men, she rode home to the open arms of her family.

When Mulan neared the family's qionglu, it was Yaoer who saw his sister first. Now a strapping lad of seventeen, he was the same age as Mulan had been when she'd left to join the Great Khan's army.

"Mulan is home! Mulan is home!" Yaoer called out.

"Brave daughter, you are home at last," Hua Hu called out, stepping out of the qionglu.

Mulan saw how her father had aged. Bowing to him respectfully, she said, "Yes, Father, your daughter has returned, having served in the Great Khan's army for twelve years."

"Your mother and I are so proud of you, Daughter. Let us celebrate and thank Od Ana for bringing you home safely," Hua Hu said, gesturing for Mulan to come into the tent.

The troop of male soldiers behind Mulan looked at each other in surprise.

"Daughter?" one of them asked.

"We travelled and fought together for twelve years, and yet we didn't know that Mulan was a woman. How could that be?" another continued, baffled.

"Brothers-in-arms, when two hares run together side by side, can you tell which one is the male and which the female?" Mulan asked as she pulled off her boots. And with that, she ran barefoot through the grassland of her home, like she used to do when she was a young girl living in the steppes.

Approaching Mudan's paddock, she called out, "I am home at last!"

She took off her warrior's helmet to let her hair, now regrown, flow freely down her back. Ahead of her, Mudan neighed in excitement on hearing her rider's voice once again.

MOMOTARO, THE PEACH BOY

This story of a boy called Momotaro, who was born from a peach, has to be one of Japan's most renowned folktales. It is said to have been spread through oral storytelling during the Muromachi period (1392 to 1573). The story was then printed during the Edo period (1603 to 1867) when Japan was ruled by a military government, the Tokugawa shogunate, and feudal lords called daimyo, and arts and culture flourished. Since then, children in Japan have been able to read this folktale. Many variations of Momotaro exist, and this is one retelling.

A long time ago in Okayama, Japan, there lived a man and his wife. Although they did not have much money, they had many things going for them – good health, enough to eat and a love so strong that even the Heavens wept. There was only one thing they wanted as a married couple but could not have.

"Grant us a child, O Heavens above," the wife prayed, longing to hold a baby in her arms.

"Give us a baby, O Heavens above, so we don't die without kin," the husband prayed, hoping for a son to pass on his family name.

The couple visited their village temple daily and prayed to Inari, the Goddess of Fertility, for a baby. They did this for many years. But for many years, no child came.

As the years went by, the chances of bearing children grew smaller and smaller until the hope for a child disintegrated into dust that collected around the woman's heart.

Then, one day, the wife – who had now grown old – felt a craving so strong she could not ignore it.

"Husband, I have an urge to eat sweet peaches," she told her husband. "Please can you find me some?"

"Wife, peaches are not in season right now," he replied. "But a sudden food craving out of season like this can only mean one thing. Are you with child?" he asked in hope.

"I'm nearing sixty, Husband, and I'm too old to bear a child now," his wife said with a heavy sigh. "And yet my body craves for the juice and flesh of the momo."

With his heart brimming with deep love for his wife, the husband set out in search of peaches.

"Be careful the oni doesn't get you, Husband," his wife warned. "You'll be going into the woodland where there are caves. It is said that these monsters are cave dwellers, and they wait for innocent humans to walk by their home so they can devour them."

She knew that the oni, who were ogre-demons, were cruel and dangerous, and once they had ensnared you, it would take a powerful magic, or a very strong person, to set you free.

"Don't worry, Wife," her husband reassured her, gulping down his fear. "Oni are nothing but monsters made up to scare children."

But he did not quite believe it. However, it was said that there was an island not far from them, where the oni king had his lair. But nobody had ever come back alive to tell the tale.

"Husband, I'm *sure* that oni live in caves, and there

is an ancient cave in the woodland," his wife replied. "Here, take this bag of beans to ward off the evil oni."

So, tucking the bag of beans into his obi-belt, the husband went on his way.

To get to the nearest peach tree in the woods, he did indeed have to walk past an ancient cave. As he passed, he removed the bag of beans from his belt and scattered a handful at the mouth of the cave, then scurried away as fast as he could. Feeling a little more secure that he had warded off the evil oni, he whistled as he wound his way past a row of cherry blossom trees and made his way towards the peach tree.

"Ah, it is lovely to be walking in the woods. Just look at the sakura with their pretty pink petals." He stopped under a tree to gaze up at its blooms. He felt the urge to say a prayer as a pink petal floated to the ground.

The husband prayed for a miracle because he knew that peaches did not grow in spring. They were more of a summer fruit, and the ripe ones were only good for picking from June. But, ever an optimist, he crossed his fingers that he would be able to find at least one ripe peach for his wife, and he continued walking.

Stopping by the river to quench his thirst, he

spotted a round object floating towards him. The husband squinted his eyes to peer at it, and he saw that the object was a giant fuzzy peach.

"Oh my! A peach granted to us by the Heavens! A miracle!" the husband cried, and he waded towards the peach. He picked up the huge fruit with both hands and a whiff of peachy perfume made his stomach rumble. "Thank you, Heavens, for granting my prayers!"

Carrying the peach carefully, the man rushed home in his wet kimono, excited to present the fruit to his wife.

She was surprised and delighted by his gift. "Husband, where did you find this big pink peach?" the wife said as she prepared to cut up the fruit for eating.

But then, as she sliced into the peach, a small voice cried out, "Be careful where you put that knife!"

Stepping back in shock, the wife asked, "Who speaks?"

She was greeted by a gurgling laugh as the peach split open and a little boy leaped out from its centre, smiling broadly.

"I speak, Okakasama," the little boy greeted the woman, calling her Mother.

"Who are you?" asked the husband.

"I am your son granted to you by the Heavens above, Ototosama," the little boy said, calling the man Father. "Do not be afraid of me! I am no demon or monster."

The old couple bowed in gratitude to the Heavens.

Turning to his son, the husband said, "We will name you *Momo* because you were born from a peach and *taro* because you're the eldest son: Momotaro."

From that day onwards, they became good parents to the boy, and the family of three were happy and contented. Momotaro grew up to be a strong and generous child. He could lift logs with his bare hands from the time he could walk, and in this way he could be a great help to his father when their wooden house needed repairing.

Momotaro also had a kind heart and a great love for his mother, helping her around the house with sweeping, cleaning and cooking. He ground millet into flour for kibi-dango, the sweet millet dumplings that were his favourite food. Momotaro was also very good with animals, and looked after the family's chickens and koi carps well.

Life was good until one day, when Momotaro

was fifteen years old, a band of gruesomely greedy and awfully brutish oni decided to terrorize his village. The terrible oni stole the villagers' animals and depleted their rice and millet store, leaving the people hungry. They disrupted the tranquillity in the village by rampaging through the streets, shouting rude words and destroying everything in their path. The villagers were so scared for their children that they kept them indoors, so none of them played outdoors any more.

"Okakasama, Ototosama, I want to put a stop to the ogre-demons bullying us," Momotaro told his parents. "Children used to laugh and play, but now there is only a sad silence and fear surrounding our village."

Of course, Momotaro's parents were worried, and they did not want him to go. But their brave son persuaded his parents to change their minds by reassuring them that he had the strength and power to beat the oni.

"I wonder where the oni live," Momotaro said. "Ototosama, Okakasama, do you know?"

Momotaro's mother paused to think for a while, then she replied, "I heard that there is an island not far from here – Onigashima. The island is known as Demon Island, because that's where the evil oni king lives. There's a demon cave where he has his lair, and I heard that, in this cave, treasures of gold and gems are piled high, and his minion oni guard the treasures with their lives."

"Then this is where I'll go," Momotaro announced to his parents. "After I've defeated the oni leader and his minions, I shall bring some treasure home to share with everyone in our village. It is unjust that the oni should hoard so much treasure and still steal everything we have."

"You are a brave boy, my son, but nobody who has gone there has ever returned," Momotaro's mother said, her face sagging with worry.

"I'm strong and I'm not afraid. I will return, Okakasama," Momotaro assured his mother.

"With what's left of our millet supply, I'll make you some kibi-dango to take with you, for I don't want you to fight the demons on an empty stomach," she said. "I will also give you a bag of beans to throw at the evil oni king."

"If you were not a son born from a peach, sent to us by the Heavens, I'd stop you from going to Onigashima," Momotaro's father said. "But you are a strong young man, so I will give you my blessings. I know that you'll defeat the oni king."

The next day, as the sun was just beginning to rise in the sky, Momotaro prepared to set off on his adventure with his bento box of kibi-dango wrapped up in a cloth sack, and the bag of beans tucked in his obi-belt. He tied the sack across his shoulders, bade his parents farewell and went on his way.

"*To Onigashima I will go, I will go, I will go, with my bento box of kibi-dango. And the oni king I will slay, I will slay, I will slay, and his treasures I will bring back home, bring back home, bring back home,*" Momotaro sang as he made his way towards Demon Island by foot.

It was soon midday and Momotaro stopped for a rest under a tall ginkgo tree. He unpacked his bento box and took out one kibi-dango. He was just about to take a bite of it when a sheepdog bounded towards him, barking madly.

"You are trespassing, young man. This is my territory, and nobody goes through here without permission, and without feeding me. I will bite you if you don't hand over all your kibi-dango at once!" the sheepdog growled, baring his sharp canine teeth at Momotaro.

Momotaro was unfazed. Instead, he giggled good-naturedly and told the sheepdog exactly who he was.

"I am Momotaro, demon-slayer, slave to no dog,

master of myself, and a friend to all. Kibi-dango is my favourite food, and I will share some with you if you come with me to fight the oni king and his minions. I'm sure you'll scare the ogre-demons off with your loud bark."

When the sheepdog heard that Momotaro was a demon-slayer, he bowed his head until it touched the ground, and begged Momotaro to forgive him for being so insolent.

Momotaro laughed once more and threw some kibi-dango to the sheepdog. It gobbled up the millet dumpling in one go, and they both set off towards Onigashima, the island of demons.

Soon after, they came to a dell, where cedar trees grew. A monkey, who was resting in one of the trees, hopped to the ground when he saw the pair.

"Oi, you two, I know where you're heading. The only way to Onigashima is through this wooded dell of cedars. I want to come along too, for I've always wanted to go to Demon Island to fight the oni king and his minions."

When the sheepdog heard this, he woofed in a mocking tone at the monkey. "What would a useless monkey like you do on Onigashima? My friend Momotaro and I don't need you!"

"Well, if you don't let me come with you, I'll scratch your eyes out!" the monkey screeched back.

After the monkey had said this, a squabble ensued between the monkey and the sheepdog.

Momotaro watched in amusement and said, "Monkey, you are very brave to want to join us on our quest. Your courage is what we'll need in slaying the oni king and his minions. Have some kibi-dango, and then come with us."

The sheepdog reluctantly left the monkey alone. Then, after the monkey ate up the kibi-dango, the trio set off towards their destination.

They soon came to a field of tall grass. Circling above them was a pheasant, who flew down to take a better look at the boy and his two animal companions. The pheasant landed by Momotaro's feet, and Momotaro noticed that the bird was wearing a red crown and its body was covered by five rows of different coloured feathers – green, blue, golden brown, violet and red – that shimmered in the sun.

"How beautiful you are, Pheasant," Momotaro said. "But with your sharp beak, you are powerful."

On hearing this, Sheepdog felt a stab of jealousy in his chest. He barked loudly and ran after the pheasant, who flapped its wings and took flight.

When the sheepdog turned round to return to Momotaro's side, the pheasant swooped down, grabbed the dog's tail in its beak and yanked it hard.

The dog yelped in pain, and Momotaro threw some kibi-dango at the bird. "Eat this instead, Pheasant, and leave Sheepdog alone. Come and join us in our adventure to Onigashima."

The monkey was not happy to see that Momotaro was giving the pheasant so much attention, and he began to quarrel with Pheasant. The two animals shouted abuse at each other, and the sheepdog, who loved a good fight, joined in too. The ruckus was deafening, so Momotaro put his fingers to his lips and whistled loudly to catch their attention.

"Animals, you are being terribly silly," Momotaro said, once they had stopped their squabbling. "You are not each other's enemies. Remember that we are fighting a common enemy – the oni king! And united we stand, divided we fall."

When everybody was at peace with each other again, Momotaro led the way towards the island where the oni's lair stood. When they reached the edge of a body of water – the north-eastern sea – Momotaro made a raft to sail with his troop of three soldiers to Onigashima.

The oni's cave was at the top of a tall hill on the island, and when they had crossed the sea safely the four friends started to climb up the hill.

As they approached the mouth of the oni king's cave, a rumbling noise echoed from within the cave's walls and their noses picked up the stench of rotting fish. Monkey gagged from the foul odour. Sheepdog, who didn't mind bad smells, sniffed around and led Momotaro and the troop into the cave. Pheasant flew towards the thunderous din to look out for potential danger.

"I don't see any monsters. I'm sure the oni king must be deep inside the cave," Pheasant reported as he flew back to his friends. "If we take down the strongest of them all, it would weaken his army."

"Pheasant is right," Momotaro said. "Let's find the oni king and slay him."

As they crept their way deep into the cave, Momotaro saw the band of oni that had terrorized his village and his neighbours. Some were hairy, while others had horns and fangs. There were green-coloured ones and mustard-yellow ones. No matter their colour and features, all of them looked terrifying. And the biggest and strongest of them all was a red bull-faced demon. Momotaro knew instantly that this oni was the king.

Luckily, all twelve oni were passed out in a stupor, their snores echoing throughout the cave. With the demon-monsters sleeping soundly, Momotaro and his animal friends had an advantage over them.

"Oh, how noisy the oni are even when they're fast asleep," said Sheepdog to Momotaro in disgust.

Meanwhile, Monkey screeched to show that he too could make noise, and Pheasant thumped Monkey on the nose with a wing. "Shush, you silly monkey, before you wake the awful creatures up." With this, Monkey bounded at Pheasant to attack her.

Momotaro jumped up and down, waving his arms to get his friends' attention. "Shhhh! They are the enemies, remember?" Momotaro whispered urgently, gesturing at the drooling oni.

Just at this moment, the oni king woke up with a start. He snorted in shock to see Momotaro and the animals inside his cave, and he opened his mouth wide and shouted, "Wake up! Wake up! We have been invaded!"

The oni king stumbled to his feet as several of his monstrous minions woke up, and immediately started to battle the troop of four.

Pow! Wallop! Bang! Momotaro whacked each one

of the minions hard on their heads, making them see stars.

"YOU!" roared the oni king in rage, pointing at Momotaro with a knobbly, clawed finger.

As Momotaro dusted his hands, Pheasant swooped in and pecked the red bull-faced demon on his head, Sheepdog bit his hairy legs, and Monkey scratched his bulbous eyes, blinding him immediately.

Then Momotaro used his great strength to drag the screaming oni king out of the cave. He lifted the monstrous creature up with all his might and threw him into the frothing sea below. The rest of the demons, now wide awake, cowered in fright at the might of Momotaro and the loss of their king. The boy and his troop of three took their chance. They rounded up the ogre-demons and threw them, one by one, into the sea.

The last thing that was heard on Onigashima was the roar of the oni king and the howling and yelping of his eleven minions as they fell headlong into the choppy waters. At this moment, Momotaro remembered the bag of beans his mother had given him. He knew they were to ward off evil, and so he took out the bag from his obi-belt and emptied the beans into water below.

"Good riddance for ever, evil oni," Momotaro said, as he dusted his hands and wiped them on his kimono.

After defeating the oni king and his army, the four friends went deeper into the cave. Pheasant flew ahead once more, exploring the cavernous place, and finally she came upon the chamber, where the piles of treasure were kept.

"Over here," Pheasant called. "I have found the treasure!"

Momotaro clapped in glee. He quickly filled his bento box with as many gemstones and as much gold as it could contain. Then all four friends made tracks to return to Momotaro's village.

As they crossed the sea, they sang, "*The oni king we have slayed, we have slayed, we have slayed. And treasures we have found, we have found, we have found.*"

When they arrived home, there was a feast of kibi-dango awaiting them. The villagers cheered and clapped, and Momotaro's parents could not have been more proud of their son for freeing them all from the threat of the oni.

As for the treasure, Momotaro did as he had promised – he gave every villager a precious gemstone and nobody had to live in poverty again.

From then on, everyone in the village lived in peace as the oni king and his minions never returned to pillage and terrorize them. For this, the village chief made Momotaro a village hero, and he also declared that kibi-dango would always be the special food eaten to celebrate the bravery of Momotaro and his friends.

ANCIENT LOVE STORIES

The following quartet of stories, filled with mystery, miracles and magic, form the fabric of the legendary Four Folktales. In these stories you will read about immortals meddling in the romantic lives of human beings, ordinary people falling in love with animal spirits or goddesses, and the things that humans are willing to do and endure for the sake of love. These stories reflect the way the East Asians have viewed human relationships and romantic love over the centuries.

CHANG'E, HOUYI AND THE MID-AUTUMN FESTIVAL

Chang'e and Houyi are household names wherever you find people of Chinese heritage. Their story is linked to the Mid-Autumn Festival, or Zhongqiu Jie, a celebration second in importance only to the Chinese New Year. Sometimes known as the Mooncake Festival, the Full Moon Festival or Harvest Moon Festival, it is celebrated on the fifteenth day of the eighth lunar month, which falls between late September and early October. The earliest record of this festival dates back more than three thousand years, and it gained popularity during the Tang dynasty

(618 to 907 CE), when Emperor Xuanzong started to celebrate it in his palace.

In Vietnam the festival is known as Tết Trung Thu. A variant known as Tsukimi is celebrated in Japan, and in Korea it is known as Chuseok. These countries celebrate the festival on the same day as the Chinese, since they also follow a lunar calendar, but they each follow their own unique rituals. There are several origin stories of how Chang'e became the Moon Goddess, adored by billions of East Asian people. This retelling is another version.

A long, long time ago in ancient China, gods and humans lived together in peace and harmony. At this time, there were ten sunbirds that brightened up the sky. They were the sons of Xihe, the Sun Goddess, and her husband, Emperor Dijun, who was a supreme deity. Xihe loved her sons very much, and every morning she would make her way to the eastern edge of the world, where the sunbirds slept, swaddled inside their gigantic wings, in a divine tree known as the Fusang tree. From a distance, they looked like ten orange blossoms hanging from the branches. The Fusang tree was said to be the beacon that called the sunbirds back to the east every night. Hence, these sunbirds were also known as the Sunbirds of Fusang.

Every morning, Xihe plucked her sons from their slumber and took all ten of them to the Eastern Lake for their daily bath. She cleaned them under their necks, scrubbed their clawed feet, and wiped their wings patiently until their feathers shimmered. Then she chose which of her children would be the sun for the day, and placed him on a magical dragon-drawn chariot. The dragon would fly the chariot across the sky so that the sunbird could shine his light upon Earth. As soon as the Dragon Chariot took off, Xihe would take her other nine sons back to the Fusang tree.

"Your turn will come, my beautiful sons," Xihe whispered as she placed each son back on the tree's branches, one by one. "Now, go back to sleep for now, and your brother will join you again tonight, when he returns from the western edge."

At the end of the day, when the Dragon Chariot had crossed over to the western edge of the world, the sunbird indeed flew back to the east and went to sleep on the Fusang tree as the moon began to appear. The next morning, Xihe would come again to bathe all ten of her sons.

"You fuss over them too much," Emperor Dijun would scold his wife.

"Emperor-husband," Xihe would reply, "they are the only sons we have, and if I don't fuss over them, who will?"

Emperor Dijun would frown and shake his head. He knew that a mother's love for her children was greater than a husband's annoyance at his wife. And so Emperor Dijun decided to leave things be.

During this time, a man named Houyi lived on Earth with his wife, Chang'e. Houyi was known for his archery skills, and Chang'e was renowned for her delicious cakes that were round and fat like the full moon – pearly white on the outside, with a sweet red-bean paste on the inside. The cakes were soft and creamy, and just one bite brought contented sighs to the person lucky enough to eat them. Chang'e only made these cakes when the moon was full.

"I wish you would always be round and bright," Chang'e said as she gazed upon the moon's face. On the moon's surface, she could see the shape of a rabbit stirring a pot.

"I wish I could be that fluffy rabbit," Chang'e said. "I wish I could live in the Moon Palace like her."

Chang'e's friends started calling her cakes "moon cakes" because they looked fat like the full moon.

Chang'e and Houyi were blessed with more than enough to eat. Emperor Dijun, the supreme deity, would bestow extra blessings on Houyi for being so skilled in archery.

"I will give you the title of Lord Archer, Houyi," Emperor Dijun said. "You will have the authority to take down the sun, if you so wish!"

Emperor Dijun made such a bold declaration to express his trust in Houyi, but he did not expect his sons, the Sunbirds of Fusang, to ever truly be at risk.

Who would dare to shoot down the sun, and why would anyone want to?

Meanwhile, Houyi marvelled at the might of the sun that shone on Earth every day. He knew of the sacred ritual that had continued for many, many millennia – he knew that Xihe the Sun Goddess bathed her sons every day and chose the one who would be the sun for the day. Houyi appreciated that the radiant sun always gave enough warmth and heat, and when night fell, the sunbird would fly back home to the eastern edge of the world. While the sunbirds slept, Houyi and Chang'e would gaze at the moon, drinking in the moonlight, happy that all was right with the world. They knew that the next day, another bird would be selected to be the sun, and everything would go on as it always had.

That was until one particular day when one of the sunbirds grew tired of the routine, and suggested that they play a trick on their mother.

"Tomorrow, let's all hop on the Dragon Chariot and brighten up the sky for the day," said the eldest of the sunbirds. "It would be such fiery fun!"

The next day, when Xihe had bathed all ten of her sons, chosen one to be the sun for the day and put him on the Dragon Chariot, his brothers flapped their wings at once and flew into the chariot, just as the dragon took flight.

Xihe was horrified. "Come back at once, my sons! There can only be one sun in the sky!"

Her nine sons ignored her, and the Dragon Chariot flew across the sky with ten sunbirds blazing. This caused the Earth to become far too hot. The tips of tall trees caught fire. The long steppe grasses charred. The world that Chang'e and Houyi knew became scorched by fire, and everyone on Earth wondered what had happened.

"Husband," Chang'e said that morning, her brows furrowing in concern. "It is extremely hot today. Look yonder and you can see the forest burning. What is happening?"

"Goodness!" Houyi replied, shading his eyes. "You're right, Wife! There is a fire raging in the Forest of Mesmerizing Murmurs. The pine trees are burning. I must do something about it."

Houyi called out to Emperor Dijun. "Emperor Dijun! I think your son is playing havoc in the sky. You must do something about it before the Earth burns to cinders."

Emperor Dijun heard the Lord Archer call to him. He looked out of his window down at Earth and saw the devastation that Houyi was talking about. He summoned Xihe to enquire about the matter.

"Emperor-husband, I'm afraid that all our ten sons are in the sky at once," Xihe said, covering her face in shame. "What shall we do?"

Emperor Dijun's face grew red with anger. "What did I say about indulging the boys too much?"

Wasting no time, Emperor Dijun flew down to Earth to see Houyi, his chosen archer.

"Houyi, never did I think that one day I would have to remind you of the authority you have – the authority to shoot down the sun," Emperor Dijun said to Houyi. "As the Lord Archer, you must do what you have to do. The Earth is dying as my naughty sons blaze mightily in the sky. Only your magic arrows can destroy them."

"Emperor-husband, wait!" Xihe cried, arriving on Earth in her cloud chariot. "Houyi cannot destroy every one of our sons. He must leave one so that there will be a sun every day to shine his light on Earth. As the Sun Goddess, this is my command."

Xihe wept as she finished her sentence. Her heart ached for the imminent loss of her other sons. She loved all ten sons equally, but their fates were now in the hands of the Lord Archer, Houyi.

Moving swiftly, Houyi took down nine of the sunbirds with his arrows, until only one was left. The Earth cooled down immediately, returning to the temperature that the people were used to. Xihe embraced the one son she had left, and the mother and son became the single sun that brightens the sky every day.

Looking down from Mount Kunlun, a magical mountain that connects the Sky and Earth, was Xiwangmu Niangniang, the Mother Goddess of the West. In her abode on this mountain, which was only accessible by immortals and deities, she had a garden where long-life peaches grew. She saw how Houyi saved the world from burning, and she decided to reward him with an elixir, a potion she concocted from her divine peaches, that would make him live for ever. She floated down to Houyi's home, where he was sharpening his arrows.

"Houyi, you are indeed the Lord Archer, skilled and precise with your arrows," Xiwangmu Niangniang said, holding the hollowed-out calabash containing the potion in her hands. "As I am the Goddess of Life and Death, Creation and Destruction, I am gifting you with this elixir of longevity. An archer with your talent should live for ever, so you can continue to protect the Earth."

"Honourable Xiwangmu Niangniang, I thank you for your generosity," Houyi replied, taking the gourd-bottle from the goddess.

As Xiwangmu Niangniang returned to Mount Kunlun, Houyi shared the good news with Chang'e. She had just finished making a batch of moon cakes, for it would be a full moon that night.

"Wife, look what the Mother Goddess, Xiwangmu Niangniang, just gave us," Houyi said proudly. "It is an elixir, and whoever drinks from it will have everlasting life."

Chang'e uncapped the gourd-bottle and took a sniff of the elixir. "Oh, it smells so peachy and sweet, Husband. But this is a small gourd, and I'm afraid that it contains enough liquid only for one person."

Houyi's heart sank. "You are right, my dear wife. How could I live for ever without you?" Houyi replied, wondering what he should do. "We should hide the elixir away."

"You are right, Houyi. This potion must never fall into the wrong hands. Let's hide it here in the kitchen," Chang'e said, taking the calabash from her husband. She hid it behind a wooden panel under the altar of Zao Shen, the Kitchen God.

That night the couple enjoyed Chang'e's freshly made moon cakes in their back garden, washing them down with fragrant tea while they gazed at the full moon, feeling assured that their secret was safe.

But little did they know that one of Houyi's archery students, Pangmeng, had come to look for his master that afternoon, and he had heard everything – and seen where Chang'e had hidden the potion. Pangmeng had always been envious of Houyi's skills, and he thought that by being Houyi's pupil he would soon learn to be as great as his master. Overhearing the couple's conversation, he knew that the elixir of longevity would be just the magic drink he needed to become greater than Houyi.

Just as Pangmeng entered the couple's kitchen to steal the potion of long life, Chang'e returned from the back garden to refill the teapot. She was startled by Pangmeng's presence, and in her surprise the teapot fell crashing to the floor.

Pangmeng, shocked by the noise and at seeing Chang'e, dropped the calabash. Instinctively, Chang'e leaped forward and caught the precious potion before it could touch the ground and be spilled. As quick as lightning, Chang'e guzzled down the peach-flavoured potion before Pangmeng could stop her.

As soon as she had swallowed the last drop of potion, she ran to Houyi in the garden.

"Houyi," she called out, "I have done something terrible!"

The moment she said this, she felt light on her feet and, instead of running, she found herself hovering above the floor. Then, before she was able to reach her husband, Chang'e started to float up, up and up, like an untethered balloon.

"Chang'e, my beautiful wife!" Houyi called to her, stretching out his hand to try to pull his wife back down to earth. "Where are you going?"

Chang'e cried out in anguish as she continued to float higher and higher towards the full moon. Houyi shot one of his arrows, in the hope of pinning Chang'e to the sky, to stop her from floating further away from him. But the magical potion that Chang'e had drunk was stronger than Houyi's mighty arrow. Nothing could stop Chang'e as she continued to drift off, as if carried by a draught, further away from Earth and higher up in the sky. She soon disappeared from sight, until only her shadow could be seen on the moon's full face.

That night, the fifteenth day of the eight lunar month, Houyi and Chang'e were forever separated. After this, the only way for Houyi to gaze at his wife's beautiful face again was on the night of a full moon.

Houyi's longing for Chang'e was shared by his friends and family, who all missed her deeply. Seeing how sad Houyi had become over the months, they decided to urge Houyi to remember his wife on the anniversary of her disappearance, and to honour her by eating moon cakes while gazing upon the moon's lovely face. They told Houyi that Chang'e was living in the Moon Palace with her pet rabbit and that she would find a way to reunite with him.

Soon, the people of ancient China developed a ritual to honour Chang'e annually on the fifteenth day of the eighth month. Family and friends would come together in memory of a woman named Chang'e, who sacrificed her time on Earth with her husband so that the elixir of immortality would not fall into the wrong hands, and they made her their moon goddess.

Over the years they would continue to gather on that special day, and they too believe that Chang'e is still trying to reunite with Houyi. Because the anniversary of Chang'e's voyage to the moon takes place midway through autumn, the festival has come to be known as the Mid-Autumn Festival, or Zhongqiu Jie.

If you peer at the moon on the fifteenth day of the eighth lunar month, when the moon is at its fullest and brightest, you will catch a glimmer of Chang'e's shadow. Some say that she is stirring a pot with the rabbit on the moon, brewing an elixir to bring Houyi, her husband, to the Moon Palace to be with her.

As for Xihe, she was glad that the people of ancient China had a moon goddess they could worship. With both a sun goddess and a moon goddess, the sun-yang energy would be balanced by the moon-yin energy. Knowing that the world was in balance, Xihe continued to bathe her only son every morning before he crossed from the eastern edge of the world to western side in his Dragon Chariot.

THE LEGEND OF LADY WHITE SNAKE

This famous legend from the Tang dynasty (618 to 907 CE) takes us back to a time in China when a man named Xu Xian fell hopelessly in love with a snake spirit named Bai Suzhen, or Lady White Snake. In this retelling, Xu Xian is reunited with his love after attempts by the monk Fahai to separate them.

The story is considered an allegory that combines the Three Teachings: Taoism, Buddhism and Confucianism. It explores the themes of love, accepting people for who they are, including their flaws, and how people's fates are linked on Earth. Over time, this legend has taken many forms, starting out as a cautionary tale of how evil can be disguised as good, evolving into a horror story about the havoc evil spirits can cause, before becoming a more uplifting story of forbidden love, separation and reunion.

The original written version of the story can be found in Cautionary Stories for the World, *a collection of novellas that was published in the mid-seventeenth century, compiled and edited by Feng Menglong, a Ming-dynasty Chinese poet, historian and novelist.*

It is believed that a long, long time ago in China, there was an ancient lake where two snake spirits dwelled. They were Lady White Snake and her sister, Lady Green Snake. The lake was not only their home, it was also their sanctuary. It was in this lake that they meditated daily, following the Taoist doctrines that would make them immortals, ensure their longevity and give them magical powers.

Lady White Snake meditated for one thousand years, and in this time she was bestowed with powerful magic from the Universe: she was able to turn herself into a human woman. She took the form of a beautiful maiden at the prime of her youth.

But Lady Green Snake did not have the same power.

"Come on, Sister Green Snake," Lady White Snake said. "Just concentrate a bit more, and you will become human too."

"But, Sister White Snake, I didn't meditate for as long as you did. My magic isn't as strong," Lady Green Snake replied, desperately trying to transform herself.

"You can do it! Will it, and it shall happen," said Lady White Snake.

Finally, with much perseverance and determination, Lady Green Snake transformed herself into a human girl.

"There you go, Sister Green Snake – I knew you could do it! Now, we need names to call ourselves. I will be Bai Suzhen, and you, little sister, will be Xiaoqing," Lady White Snake said. "We will put our serpentine lives behind us, and from today we'll behave like proper humans, with kindness and dignity."

Then the two sisters left their lake home and travelled to Hangzhou, a city in the eastern part of the country. Being former water serpents, they followed their instincts to a body of water, which was called West Lake.

Bai Suzhen marvelled at their new surroundings, taking in the lay of the land and soaking in the beauty of nature. She noticed that some distance away, on the other side of West Lake, was a pagoda. She spied a monk in his golden-orange robe sitting cross-legged, meditating, at the foot of the pagoda, and this pleased her.

"A pagoda is a sign that this is a place of spiritual importance," Bai Suzhen said to Xiaoqing. "And a meditating monk is a joyful sight to behold."

"Then let us build our home here, Elder Sister," suggested Xiaoqing.

Bai Suzhen closed her eyes and meditated for a few minutes, and bags of ingots formed around her feet. With the money, she bought a small piece of land opposite the pagoda, across the lake. She made sure that a thicket of pine trees obscured the house's view, to give the meditating monk some privacy.

Then, Bai Suzhen sent Xiaoqing on an errand. The younger lady was to seek out several handymen and carpenters and employ them to build a new house by the shores of the West Lake.

When their home was ready, Bai Suzhen and Xiaoqing moved in immediately. They employed several servants and paid a seamstress to dress them like noblewomen. And, like noblewomen, the two ladies also learned needlework and calligraphy, and when they were not occupied with these activities, they passed the time each day in tranquil meditation or walking in the forests around West Lake, where they foraged for herbs to make teas and broths.

Soon the summer months turned to autumn, and autumn to winter. As the days became colder, they warmed their stomachs with herbal broths and lukewarm sweet tangyuan soups. Tangyuan in sweetened water was Xiaoqing's favourite; she loved the sticky-rice balls filled with black sesame most. Bai Suzhen savoured the ones filled with peanut paste.

"Xiaoqing, it's about time we paid our neighbour, the meditating monk, a visit," Bai Suzhen said one fine wintry morning. "As today is the Dongzhi Festival, the start of the winter solstice, it is a good time to bring a bowl of warm tangyuan soup for our neighbour. The winter solstice is when we remember friends and family, and since we have no family but each other, we should make new friends, who can be like family. The monk will appreciate our gesture."

The pair set off with a porcelain container of sweet sticky-rice balls in warm sugary water, walking the short distance to the pagoda along a curved path that hugged the lake. There, they were greeted by the meditating monk, who introduced himself as Fahai.

"Welcome to Leifeng Pagoda, my humble home," Fahai said, gesturing for the two sisters to enter.

"Have some tangyuan soup, Venerable Fahai," Bai Suzhen said, scooping the dessert into a small ceramic bowl for the monk.

When Fahai took the bowl from Bai Suzhen, he gasped in shock. On the surface of the clear soup, swimming with pink and white sticky-rice balls, Fahai thought he saw the face of a white snake reflected back at him.

"What is the matter, honourable monk?" Bai Suzhen asked.

"N-nothing," Fahai stuttered a reply, puzzled. He caught Bai Suzhen's eyes and looked into them intently.

I must be mistaken, Fahai thought to himself. He shook off the foreboding feeling and swallowed a spoonful of delicious sweet soup. He bit into a pink rice ball, filled with peanut paste, and his lips curled into a slight smile. *I must hide my true feelings*, Fahai said to himself, and he made his smile broader.

Pleased, Bai Suzhen nodded at her sister, and Xiaoqing served a bowl of tangyuan to her sister, before preparing one for herself.

The neighbours ate their winter dessert in silence, savouring the different tangyuan fillings oozing from the rice balls. But while the two sisters were happy, Fahai was far from contented. That initial feeling of dread kept niggling away at him, so even the sweet tangyuan soup started to taste a little bitter at the end. He finished his bowl quickly and made a polite excuse, saying that he needed to return to his meditation. The two sisters packed up their bowls and utensils and left for home.

"Oh, what a lovely monk – though he could've let us stay a bit longer," Xiaoqing said as they arrived home.

But Bai Suzhen was a little more disappointed than Xiaoqing.

On the same day, as fate would have it, a man named Xu Xian bought a bowl of tangyuan from a vendor who had set up shop by Broken Bridge, near West Lake.

The vendor was none other than Lü Dongbin, the Scholar Immortal – one of the Eight Immortals who'd made their homes on five islands in the Bohai Sea, not far from a sacred mountain called Mount Penglai. Immortals may be divine beings, some with lofty aspirations like Lü Dongbin, but they are not lacking in imagination, nor immune to the urge to playing the odd trick. Lü Dongbin had grown bored of writing poetry in his studio on Mount Penglai, and thought it would be fun to pretend to be humans for the day.

Xu Xian ate his delicious tangyuan soup, and for the next three days he did not feel hungry at all. Curious to know why, he returned to the bridge to ask the vendor.

"I'm the Immortal, Lü Dongbin," the vendor confessed, laughing at Xu Xian. "Those were immortality pills that you ate in your tangyuan soup."

"Why would you give me immortality pills?" Xu Xian asked, aghast. "I'm surely not worthy of enlightenment. I've not meditated for long enough yet."

"I wanted to know what would happen if a human took them, and now I know," the Immortal answered, chuckling loudly. "Here, let me help you get rid of them."

He picked Xu Xian up, took him to the shores of West Lake and tipped him upside down. Then he jiggled Xu Xian up and down as though he was emptying a sack of potatoes, and out tumbled all the rice balls that Xu Xian had eaten three days ago. After the last of the immortality pills plopped into the lake, Lü Dongbin dropped Xu Xian on the grassy edge and disappeared in a puff of smoke, his laughter echoing in the wintry air.

Bai Suzhen happened to be gazing out of her bedroom window when Lü Dongbin tipped poor Xu Xian upside down. Curious, she decided to take a closer look at what was happening – but she left her home before she could see Lü Dongbin vanishing into thin air, the way he did.

By the time she arrived at the lake's edge and found the dazed Xu Xian, she also found herself alone with this handsome young man.

"Are you all right?" she asked the man, helping him to his feet.

As he stood and faced her, the kind contours of his face quickened her heart.

When Xu Xian set his eyes on Bai Suzhen, his heart also skipped several beats, and he knew at once this was the woman he wanted to make his wife. Behind her gleaming black eyes, he saw intelligence. There was a genteel quality about the woman, as well as a gentle manner that he found soothing.

"Maiden, I'm Xu Xian, and I'm pleased to make your acquaintance," Xu Xian said to the blushing Bai Suzhen. "I'll be honest with you, I've never felt the way I do right now about anyone before. One day, I'd like to make you my wife, if you're willing to marry me."

"Sir, I'm honoured at your proposal," Bai Suzhen replied. "Come into my humble home, and warm yourself there."

And so it was that Bai Suzhen and Xu Xian came to live together, and they shared this home with Xiaoqing, who was over the moon that her sister had found such a trustworthy man to share her life and home with.

Several months later, Bai Suzhen and Xu Xian decided to make their union official. They would have a small wedding, they decided – only the most important people would be invited. The first person who they thought to invite as an honoured guest to their wedding was Fahai, the monk.

Bai Suzhen penned a poem in a written invitation to the monk. Xu Xian and Bai Suzhen then delivered the invitation personally to Fahai. But instead of being pleased for the couple, their neighbour opposed the marriage immediately. The reason he gave was that their union was unnatural.

"What are you talking about, Venerable Fahai?" asked Bai Suzhen. "You know that this cannot be true. I am very much in love with Xu Xian, as he is with me. How is that unnatural?"

Xu Xian was just as confused as Bai Suzhen. "How can we prove that our union is every bit as natural as everyone else's?" he asked, as Bai Suzhen stormed out of the pagoda, infuriated by the monk's reaction.

Fahai took Xu Xian's desire to prove the legitimacy of his relationship with Bai Suzhen as a challenge. He told Xu Xian that he should find a way to see his wife's true nature. "Take a shiny surface to her face, and see what her real form looks like," Fahai told Xu Xian. "She is a lowly snake spirit, a shape-shifter! If you can still love her, then your love is true, and so you may marry her."

When Xu Xian returned home, he related to Bai Suzhen what Fahai had told him.

Bai Suzhen felt betrayed. She had tried to befriend the monk, and kindly taken him food every now and then, which he ate without complaint, always smiling. Now this same monk was meditating on how he could separate her from the man she loved and wanted to marry. Bai Suzhen's initial anger turned into a tornado of rage.

"And I thought a meditating monk was a good omen. I curse the day I met Fahai!" she screeched, and Xu Xian cowered at the force of her wrath.

She was furious that Fahai had doubted her. "*I am a woman, not a snake!*" Bai Suzhen hissed. "*I am a noblewoman, not a shape-shifter!*" she shrieked. "*I deserve respect, not contempt,*" Bai Suzhen snarled. The angrier Bai Suzhen grew, the louder she hissed. "*How dare he?*"

She opened her front door and screamed towards the pagoda, hurling every insult at Fahai that she could think of. Her tongue rattled, quivering and slithering in and out of her lips, like a cobra about to shoot venom from its fangs. The words that tumbled out of her mouth were unrepeatable, and Xu Xian saw the true colours of the woman he was about to marry. He did not need a shiny surface to do that. It was her final hiss that sent Xu Xian running, so scared of the woman he wanted to marry that he felt he could no longer face her. Xu Xian fled to another city near Hangzhou.

And so it was that Bai Suzhen and Xu Xian were separated. But, as time passed, Xu Xian calmed down, and began to reflect back. He realized that he missed Bai Suzhen. He missed her kindness, the delicious herbal broths that she made for him when he was not feeling well and her loving embrace. He decided that love would endure all, and three or four years after he'd left he returned to West Lake to tell Bai Suzhen that he could not live without her.

When he arrived at the sisters' home, he found it had burned to the ground, with only a charred pillar that used to hold up the roof remaining. He ran over to the pagoda to ask if Fahai knew what had happened.

"You must forget her, young man, for she is not a good woman," Fahai urged Xu Xian. "The woman you were about to marry is a snake! She caused the lake to flood and water poured out of it, damaging the holy Leifeng Pagado, my home. I took revenge by burning down her home. And look at what she did to me."

Fahai showed Xu Xian the snake-bite scars on his right arm. He recounted the battle that had ensued between him and Bai Suzhen. He told Xu Xian of how she and Xiaoqing had tried to poison him with a herbal tea, in a pretend gesture of reconciliation. Fahai also told Xu Xian of how the two women returned to their snake forms during the battle, showing him their true natures.

"I imprisoned them. But my magic was not strong enough to hold down two powerful female forces," Fahai concluded. "They escaped and are now in Zhenjiang."

Unfazed by all he had heard, Xu Xian decided to travel to Zhenjiang, a city not far from Hangzhou, to find Bai Suzhen.

When he arrived at Zhenjiang several days later, he asked around for news about two sisters, and an old woman directed him.

"Take this path, and you'll find a humble medicine shop," the old woman said with a toothless grin. "The older one, Lady Bai, is a herbalist, and her sister, Lady Qing, takes care of the shop. Such kind women they are. They always heal me for no money at all."

When Xu Xian arrived at the shop, the first thing he saw was Bai Suzhen with a toddler strapped to her back, pounding herbs to make a poultice.

"Bai Suzhen!" he called out.

She looked up, surprise written all over her face. "Xu Xian, I never thought I'd see you again. I thought that our child would never know her father," Bai Suzhen said, her voice cracking with emotion.

Xu Xian was moved at the sight of the daughter he did not know he had. He apologized to the woman he loved with all his heart. As he cuddled his child, Xu Xian told Bai Suzhen how for months and months he had meditated on the subject of human nature and come to the realization that there will always be those who hate, and those who love – and he wanted to be one who loved. Xu Xian said he had discovered that those who do not know love will always try to break it apart.

Then he added, "Meditating and wearing a holy colour does not make someone a better-natured person. In every human, there are parts of us that are bad, like green venom, and parts of us that are good, like medicated healing balm. We need to accept that this is the true nature of every human being. I want to be that balm to your venom, Bai Suzhen, and when I'm filled with venom, I want you to be my soothing balm."

Bai Suzhen's eyes filled with tears. "I hated you so much for leaving, Xu Xian, that for years I was bitter with resentment," she confessed. "But, no matter how angry I felt, my heart was always filled with love for you, like it was on the first day I met you. And I realized that bitterness wasn't going to bring you back to me. So I hoped that love would find a way to reunite us one day."

And thus, it came to pass that Bai Suzhen and Xu Xian were reunited, both having come to an understanding that love endures all, and that there is light and dark in each of us. They were finally able to have that small wedding they'd planned all those years ago, and the first person they invited as an honoured guest was the old lady who'd pointed Xu Xian to Bai Suzhen's herbal shop.

THE BUTTERFLY COUPLE

The tale of the butterfly couple (also known as the butterfly lovers) follows the relationship between two classmates, a boy called Liang Shanbo and a girl named Zhu Yingtai, who Liang Shanbo believes to be his male classmate. This story is said to date back to medieval China (220 to 589 CE), and some historians believe that, when it was written down, it was set in the Eastern Jin dynasty (317 to 420 CE), when women were relatively free to take part in social activities outside the home.

This folktale, filled with themes of fraternal, romantic, forbidden and star-crossed love, is often called the Chinese version of Romeo and Juliet. Similarly, it is not a happy tale, but it has so much cultural significance that it has been retold time and again over the centuries in China, Korea and Vietnam.

The sadness of the tale is lessened by a touch of comedy in certain versions, and it has been adapted into films, dances, operas and animated movies for children. Because of its important secondary themes, such as femininity versus masculinity, cross-dressing and gender identities, and female empowerment in a male-dominated society, many have said that this folktale was very radical, breaking many social conventions of its time. This retelling has tried to fill in the gaps in the most-referenced version, known as the Liang-Zhu story.

A very, very long time ago in China, when girls were expected to stay at home to do domestic work like sewing, weaving and cooking while boys were sent to school to become gentlemen-scholars and trained to work in civil service, there lived a sixteen-year-old girl named Zhu Yingtai.

She had long black hair that she plaited and twirled into a bun, fastening it with elaborate hairpins at the back of her head, according to the style of the time. When she walked, the folds of her long silk robe sashayed with her every step. When she needed to use her hands, she knew to elegantly lift the robe's flowing sleeves just a touch to show her wrist and no more, in accordance with the etiquette of the day. Under a pair of sculptured eyebrows, a pair of dark eyes glimmered with curiosity. Yingtai spent hours hiding behind the screen that separated the study area from the domestic area of their house, secretly listening to her brothers recite poetry by the great poets of that time.

"Oh, what lovely words. If only I could study too," wished Yingtai with a heavy sigh. She knew she must stay quiet so not to disrupt her elder brothers' concentration.

The Zhu family came from a relatively well-to-do

lineage. They lived in the state of Wuyue during a time of peace and prosperity, when the warring in the north had stopped. Wuyue's capital, Hangzhou, was a centre of arts and culture, and this was where Yingtai wanted to go. She wanted to study there like her brothers – like all the boys from families similar to hers.

"Father," said Yingtai one day, on entering her father's room. "Please, please may I go to the capital to study like my brothers?"

Her father looked up from his reading to see his daughter kneeling, her head bowed in respect. It broke his heart to see her in this position, begging to be allowed to be like her elder brothers. Mr Zhu had nine children, and Yingtai was his last, and the only daughter. He loved her with all his heart.

"Daughter, the blossom of my eye, get up on your feet at once," said her father kindly. "You know that this is not possible. You are a girl, and girls are simply not allowed to be schooled."

"But, Father, can't you say something to the principal? He is your friend, after all," begged Yingtai, still on her knees.

"You know that such favours are not easily at the principal's disposal, Daughter," responded her father with a big sigh. "He is not in the position to grant you a place at his school just because we are friends. A lowly girl doesn't get to be educated. This is the principle, as stipulated by our ancestors. And no matter how much I want to change the rule, I cannot."

Yingtai stood up and left her father's bed chambers, her shoulders slumped in dejection and her head bowed in disappointment.

That night, she had a vivid dream of transforming into a butterfly, carrying on her wings the hope of being free.

Three days later, after she'd had a long think, Yingtai came up with a plan. She returned to her father's bed chambers once more.

"Father, I thought about what you said. You tell me a lowly girl does not deserve an education. And yet a lowly girl became a successful emperor once. Empress Wu Zetian ruled China, managing the nation across rivers and mountains. Merciful Guanyin, who learned the Buddhist sutras with passion and care, was once a girl before she became Taihou Mazu, the Goddess of the South Sea. I have a plan, dear Father," said Yingtai, tingling with hope.

"Oh, Daughter, tell me your plan," responded Mr Zhu, giving Yingtai all his attention.

"I will go to Hangzhou dressed as a boy. This way, I will be able to study like my brothers and gain knowledge and wisdom," said Yingtai solemnly. "I will no longer be a lowly girl but a high-born boy."

Her father sat in his reading chair in silence, contemplating his daughter's argument.

In the courtyard, a pair of magpies tittered, and Yingtai could hear her brothers getting ready to leave for Hangzhou for the new school term. She waited with bated breath for her father to grant her permission to fulfil her dream, and she bowed her head in deference to him.

After some moments, Mr Zhu's guttural chuckle filled the room. "Daughter, the blossom of my eye, you have put forward an indisputable argument – and, if I may say so, an insolent one too!"

"Father, I—" said Yingtai, starting to explain further. But Mr Zhu interrupted her.

"It must be said that no girl has ever been to school dressed as a boy, but, yes, a lowly girl did become a great female emperor, as you'd pointed out. I marvel at your plan and admire your independence of mind. And I'll put my hand on my heart and say it's a brilliant idea!" replied Mr Zhu, stroking his beard.

"Father, you mean to say yes to my request?" asked Yingtai.

"Daughter, go with my blessings as another son of Zhu! You are shaped like a boy, to tell the truth," said Mr Zhu with a smile. "Learn with all your heart what your brothers are being taught, and embrace that learning, for you are certainly no ordinary girl. But when I send word for your return, you must obey."

Yingtai agreed without hesitation and returned to her bed chambers with glee. Right away, she took up a pair of sewing scissors. She glided the shiny scissors through her hair as though she was cutting a yard of fabric, and her thick black tresses fell to the floor in one clean cut. Now that her hair was shorter and more manageable, she twisted it into a topknot, the way all her brothers wore theirs. Then she went to her older brother Meng's room. He was the youngest of her brothers and the one to whom Yingtai was closest. She rummaged through his cupboard and picked an outfit for herself.

"Now I look like a son of the Zhu household," said Yingtai, satisfied with her disguise.

In her new clothes, Yingtai bounded out to the courtyard, where her brothers were leaving on horseback for Hangzhou. Meng gasped in surprise to see his sister dressed like a boy.

"What are you doing, Ying?" he asked, as Yingtai clambered on to his horse, requesting a ride to their school in Hangzhou. "I know you like learning, but surely this is forbidden?"

"Father has given me his blessings, Meng! And he has also given me instructions on what to do," Yingtai replied urgently, and with that she answered her other brothers' curious stares.

After a short pause, Peng, the oldest of the siblings, said, "Well, if this is the case, we should get going before the morning turns to day. Come on, let's go!"

Yingtai and her brothers arrived at Hangzhou a couple of hours later. The bustling city excited Yingtai as she had never seen so many people all at once before. Riding past the city centre, the Zhu siblings found their way to school.

When school started the next day, Yingtai walked confidently into class. It was a lesson on classical poetry. There, she met a boy whose name was Liang Shanbo, and the pair became friends immediately.

"I'm so glad to meet a fellow new student," said Liang Shanbo, introducing himself. "Call me Liang."

"Big brother Liang!" replied Yingtai. "You can call

me Zhu," she said, telling him to address her by her surname as he himself had done.

From that day on, Zhu and Liang became inseparable. The pair were both quick learners of poetry, Zhu because of the many years she had spent listening to her older brothers reciting poems and Liang because he'd had a head start in learning by rote.

Zhu took to calligraphy like duck to water, because her feminine hands knew how to hold the brush delicately. Embroidering tiny stitches had given her this skill. The way she held the brush in her hands made her characters fluid yet firm – the way Chinese words should look. Meanwhile Liang was adept at grinding the ink sticks on the inkstone and mixing the powder with the right amount of water so the ink was not too watery, and not too concentrated.

"Zhu, your calligraphy is exquisite," said Liang. "You must show me how you do it."

"And you must show me how to get the ink consistency right," said Zhu.

For the next three years, Zhu Yingtai and Liang Shanbo passed their days studying together, learning the wonders of literature and perfecting their calligraphy. Their friendship grew stronger and they became as thick as thieves, sharing with one another their most intimate thoughts and dreams. When the school day was over, they talked deep into the night about everything, huddled securely under their blanket in the little room they shared.

Then, one day, Zhu received a letter from home telling her to return at once. And Zhu Yingtai remembered her promise to her father – that when he summoned her, she must obey and return home for good. Her heart ached to know that she might never see Liang again, for she was determined to remain with her best friend for eternity. In her heart, she had already made him this promise, and she had secretly prayed to the Heavens to make it possible for them to be married.

"I must let him know how I truly feel, and I will betroth myself to him," said Zhu to herself. "But how can I do this without embarrassing him?"

After a night spent tossing and turning, Zhu went to see the principal's wife at the crack of dawn. She confessed everything and asked for her help and support.

"Please, Madam Principal, could you let Liang

Shanbo know that my love for him is so abundant that nothing in this world is big enough to represent it?" said Zhu. "I have an heirloom – this jade bangle. It belonged to my maternal grandmother and is part of my dowry. Please would you give this to Liang in my name and tell him that I would like to be his wife?"

"Zhu Yingtai, I've never known a love like yours: one that would make a girl break all the rules of betrothal – in fact, even all the rules of conventional education," replied the principal's wife, who was astonished at the tale, and upset with herself for never noticing that Zhu was a girl in disguise. "Go back to your family in peace and leave the bangle with me."

When the moment came to say goodbye, Zhu could not hold back her tears.

Liang embraced her. "Zhu, my sworn brother, I will visit you as soon as my studies are done. But first, let me walk you to where you need to go," he offered.

"Liang, we are like a pair of mandarin ducks, forever enjoined," said Zhu, hoping that Liang would notice the symbolism in her words. But, to her disappointment, Liang did not show any inkling that he understood her deeper feelings and her desire to marry him.

She continued, "Liang, we are faithful to one another like a married couple … who are good friends and inseparable."

"Ah, Zhu! Yes, your friendship means more to me than a wife. I cannot imagine my married life without you! Promise that when I do get married, you'll stay by my side," said Liang.

"Liang, you silly goat! You could never live your married life without me. We are forever beholden to one another," hinted Zhu.

At this, Liang simply chuckled good-heartedly. By that time, he had walked his best friend eighteen miles to her destination, where she would be picked up by her family. Still, he was none the wiser that the friend he had called Zhu for three years was really a young woman – a young woman in love with him.

"Farewell, Zhu! Keep well, my friend," said Liang, pulling Zhu towards him for a final embrace.

"Come and visit me, Liang, and I will introduce you to my sister, who is like me," said Zhu, trying to swallow her tears. "The only way we can always be together is for you to marry her and become part of my family."

Upon hearing this, Liang thumped Zhu hard on her back, causing her to choke and cough.

"Oh, brother, I'm sorry," Liang apologized. "I forget how soft you are, and that you could never take such vigorous gestures. I'll come and I'll marry your sister, so our friendship will never die. And, when we die, we will become a pair of butterflies, forever together."

With these words, Zhu Yingtai returned home, her heart bursting with love for Liang Shanbo. She pined after him, waiting for his arrival. She ticked the days off in her calendar, impatiently wondering if Liang Shanbo would ever come, so she could show him who she had been all along.

It was several months later when Liang finally turned up at her home. He was determined to keep his word to his sworn brother and eager to meet Zhu's younger sister.

But when Zhu Yingtai came to meet him, dressed in her feminine clothes once more, Liang Shanbo thought she looked too familiar. He scratched his head in confusion, a frown forming on his brow. It took him a couple of moments to finally see that the woman before him was Zhu, his classmate in Hangzhou. Liang was incredulous.

"You—" said Liang. "You are the sister that I should marry! Why didn't you tell me that you were a woman all along, Zhu?"

"My name is Yingtai. I did try to tell you on the day I left, Liang. But you didn't understand my meaning at all." Her bright eyes glistened with tears.

"Zhu… I mean Yingtai, you could've been more direct with me. Now I understand why you mentioned a pair of mandarin ducks, and that we were to be forever enjoined … and why you left me a jade bangle." He pulled out the bangle Yingtai had left with the principal's wife. "I was told to bring this to a girl who lives in the Zhu family home. All this time, it was you!"

Standing there, looking at the female figure of his friend, Liang completely understood now why Zhu felt poorly, complaining of stomach pains around the same time every month. He remembered how worried he had been for his friend, as he had thought Zhu was seriously ill. It also dawned on him why Zhu behaved in such effeminate ways compared to the rest of the boys. He remembered how he used to tease Zhu for being so feminine, chiding his friend for acting weak. Yet he was also reminded of how protective he was of Zhu when the other boys teased. Suddenly so many things about the way Zhu had behaved in the three years that they'd spent together became clear to him, including why Zhu had such a feminine first name, Yingtai. And Liang Shanbo realized that he had been in love with Zhu Yingtai all along. He had been in love with Zhu's wit, humour and passion for riddles. But he did not know this until he discovered that his best friend was the young woman Yingtai.

"Yingtai, I am very surprised to discover the truth, but I am delighted too. I'd be honoured to marry you," he said.

"But you've left it too late, Liang," said Yingtai, shaking her head.

"What do you mean?" asked Liang Shanbo, feeling very desperate. "I'm here now. Here to marry—"

"Alas, I'm to be married to a man named Ma Wencai, according to my parents' wish," explained Yingtai, fat teardrops rolling down her face.

At that moment, Liang Shanbo realized just how foolish he had been. He should have understood Zhu's hints. He should have understood who she was earlier and admitted his feelings to himself.

His heart broke into a million pieces to hear her cry inconsolably, repeating, "You've left it too late, Liang, you've left it too late!"

Liang Shanbo placed the jade bangle into Zhu Yingtai's hands, before collapsing to the ground with a broken heart.

At that very moment, the sky cracked open, and torrential rain fell on Earth. The Celestial Heavens wept in despair as Liang Shanbo faded away, full of regret and love. And, as he drew his last breath, the jade bangle he had put into Zhu's hands broke into two.

Liang Shanbo was buried at the spot where he had fallen, along with the broken jade bracelet.

And Zhu Yingtai, who could not envision a day without the love of her life, became ill with grief. She pined for Liang Shanbo every day and night, growing weaker and weaker until she, too, faded away like her love.

When her last breath left her body, she transformed into a butterfly, just like in her dream from many years ago, when she'd first begged her father to let her go to school. She flew out of the window, and there she joined another butterfly that was fluttering outside, as if waiting for her.

It is said that whenever you see two white butterflies together, you must remember the butterfly couple, Liang Shanbo and Zhu Yingtai. And you must rejoice, for they are now together, for ever.

THE COWHERD AND THE WEAVER GIRL

This legendary folktale about star-crossed love is incredibly important in China, Korea, Japan and Vietnam. This version is a retelling based on several Chinese versions of the folktale.

As a couple, Niulang and Zhinü have been depicted in East Asian art since the Han dynasty (206 BCE to 220 CE), and the story can be found in the Shijing, or Book of Songs, which is more than 2,500 years old. Even today, well-educated Chinese students are still expected to memorize its poems, which are full of idioms (chengyu) made up of four, or sometimes eight, Chinese characters. This story led to the formation of the chengyu

'Niulang Zhinü', used to refer to an enduring marriage. It even inspired the Qixi Festival, which is celebrated on the seventh day of the seventh lunar month – in August in the Gregorian calendar. It is known by many other names: Magpie Festival, Double Seventh Festival, Qiqiao Festival or Chinese Valentine's Day. The Korean festival of Chilseok is related to it, whereas in Japan it is celebrated as Tanabata, and in Vietnam as Thất Tịch.

The folktale originated during a time when the ancient Chinese worshipped the mysteries of the cosmos. In ancient China, during the Qixi Festival, girls and women prayed to the star-goddess Zhinü for her wisdom and her help with their needlework, and offered her fruit, special cakes and tea. In celebration of the cowherd Niulang, children would make garlands and hang them around the necks of their oxen and buffaloes. Today, the rituals have changed to giving flowers and chocolates and having dinner with your beloved, just like during Valentine's Day.

Niulang the cowherd sat cross-legged on the grassy patch outside his hut, leaning against his water buffalo, Niuniu, who had just laid down for the night.

Niuniu grunted, as if to wish his owner goodnight.

"Goodnight, Niuniu," said Niulang as he raised his arms over his head, settling more comfortably into the creature's side.

The buffalo grunted once more, shifting so Niulang could be more comfortable. Soon, Niuniu was breathing soft, gurgling breaths as he fell fast asleep.

As a cowherd, Niulang's job was to look after the family's precious buffalo that ploughed the land where they grew their crops. Now that his day's work was done and Niuniu was asleep, Niulang could rest and dream.

He dreamed of having a full belly. He wondered what life would be like beyond the grassy confines of his home. He gazed up at the starlit sky above him.

It had always fascinated Niulang. He wondered why the stars twinkled only at night, and how far the sky was from Earth. He thought he saw shapes in the black canvas, dotted with tiny sparkles of light – over here, a plough; over there, a sword. He contemplated the vastness of the Heavens and the smallness of himself.

We are a good fit, my buffalo and me, Niulang thought as he stargazed, *but how great it would be to have a wife to love.*

There was one particular bright star that caught Niulang's eye and, as he lay there, he wished upon it.

"Oh, wondrous, bright star, grant me a good life with lots of love," Niulang prayed.

He wished upon the star that he would find a good wife, with whom he could share his hopes and aspirations and travel far and wide on the back of Niuniu.

Meanwhile in the Heavens, a star-goddess, Zhinü, finished weaving another piece of tapestry from a galaxy of stars. She put her loom away and looked down on Earth. She saw the cowherd sitting cross-legged on the grass against his precious buffalo. She noticed how the boy looked up at her, the bright star in the sky, and she became curious about many things. What would it be like to be human? To speak to a human? To come face to face with a human boy who loved stargazing?

Most of all, she was curious to know what the starlit sky looked like from a human being's perspective. *I want to go to Earth*, she thought to herself. *But I know that my father will not approve. I must find a way to persuade Niang to let me go.*

Zhinü's father was the Jade Emperor, and he had a lot of rules about how the gods of the Celestial Heavens should behave. Her mother, whom she called Niang, was Xiwangmu Niangniang, the Mother Goddess of the West. She was the supreme goddess who was in charge of creation and destruction.

"Sisters," Zhinü called. "Come into my chamber. I have something to tell you."

Zhinü's six elder sisters gathered in her bedroom, and Zhinü told them of her plan. "Let's ask Niang for permission to go down to Earth for some time. Wouldn't it be wonderful if we could have a bath in the rivers, take long walks and feel the green grass beneath our feet?"

"Oh, how I wish we could do these things," the eldest of the sisters said. "But Niang will not agree—"

"Unless we say that we will go to Earth as human maidens," the third elder sister interrupted.

"That is a fabulous idea, Third Elder Sister," Zhinü said. "Then nobody will ever know that we are actually star-goddesses."

So, the bevy of seven sisters floated to their mother's chambers on Mount Kunlun, and each one of them tried to convince their mother why she should let them go down to Earth.

"We will be good and compliant," said the fourth sister, a people-pleaser.

"We won't make any trouble," said the fifth, who was talkative. "I suggest that only Zhinü should have words when we are in the company of humans."

"I second Fifth Sister's suggestion," said the second, who was the agreeable one. "We will look after one another."

And finally the sixth sister, who was the compassionate one, said, "Niang, we will do good while we are on Earth. We will bless the people with star-dusted harmony and star-spangled love."

It was this sister who convinced Xiwangmu Niangniang to let them go, and to keep it a secret from the Jade Emperor.

"Star-daughters, you must remember that the only way back is through your star gowns. Make sure that they're not torn or lost," cautioned Xiwangmu Niangniang. And with that, she let her daughters descend to Earth on a cloud just before the sun brightened up the sky.

When the seven sisters arrived on Earth, the world was still asleep – except for one boy and his buffalo. Niulang and Niuniu were just waking up. They had a long day ahead of them because today was market day, and Niulang's father had bags of goods that needed lugging there in the cart.

At home, Niulang splashed some cold water on his face to wake himself up. Then he broke off half of the sweet potato left over from last night's meal, saving the other half for his father, who had already gone out into the fields to work.

"Come on then, Niuniu. Let's get you to a fresh grassy patch for breakfast," Niulang said, tugging at the buffalo's horn. "Then a bath before we set off."

Niulang ate his cold breakfast while he led his bovine friend towards his own.

Soon, they came to a dewy patch of grass near the river. "Eat to your heart's content, Niuniu," Niulang said, finishing up the last of his sweet potato. "The grass looks juicy and fresh."

While Niuniu ate his morning meal, Niulang waited patiently under a baobab tree. Not long after, in the quiet of the morning, he heard the sound of giggling coming from the direction of the river. He sat upright to listen carefully, making sure that it was not the early-morning breeze rustling through the grass. The giggling changed to sing-song voices.

"How strange," Niulang said to himself. "This sounds like some girls talking. Come on, Niuniu, let's go investigate."

Niuniu was not too happy to have his leisurely breakfast interrupted, but he loved his master, and where Niulang went, he went too. He chewed his last bit of cud and lumbered off in Niulang's direction.

As they neared the river, the laughter and chatting grew clearer and louder. Peering round a tree, Niulang was surprised to see seven beautiful girls bathing in the river. He blushed at the sight. Then he noticed the girls' dresses lying in a heap at the river's edge, and his blush turned a deeper red.

Niulang did not want to seem as if he was spying, so he called out, "Good morning! Where are you from?"

Immediately, seven beautiful faces turned to look at him in surprise. "Avert your eyes!" Zhinü cried out.

At this, Niulang turned round bashfully. "I'm sorry, I didn't mean..." he started to say, but he could not find the words to continue his sentence.

"Throw us our clothes," the same voice said.

"What – into the river?" Niulang asked. "But ... that'll make them wet!"

"Never you mind, young man," the voice replied.

Niulang did as he was told and picked up the heap of gossamer clothes and threw them into the river.

"Now, shut your eyes," the girl said.

Niulang did as he was told. He heard the splashing of water, and then a long silence. Niulang eventually opened his eyes and turned to face the river. To his surprise, he saw that six of the beautiful maidens had vanished, but the seventh was standing on the bank, glaring at him. She wore her delicate gossamer gown, but one of its sleeves was missing.

"Who are you? And why did you follow us?" Zhinü asked.

"I'm Niulang, a humble cowherd. I was out feeding my buffalo, Niuniu, when I heard laughter and chatter from the river. Who are you?"

"Ahh! I know you!" Zhinü realized. Seeing the cowherd in person and hearing his name spoken out loud, she felt that she already knew him. And so, even though the seven sisters were to keep their jaunt on Earth a secret, she decided to tell him the truth, because she trusted him. "I feel I've known you all my life, Niulang. I've watched you looking up at the

Heavens every night for so long that I've yearned to come down to Earth to join you. I am Zhinü, and the girls you saw were my six sisters from the Heavens. You mustn't tell anyone who we are."

Niulang was stunned, but he knew that Zhinü was telling the truth. Her skin was milky white, Niulang noticed. She also glowed with a translucent shimmer. And before Niulang could stop himself, he found his heart tumbling with emotions he had never felt before.

"I swear your secret is safe with me, star-maiden," he said. "But where are your sisters now?"

Zhinü looked alone and forlorn. "My sisters have all returned home. I can't join them unless I find a way to weave a sleeve for my dress." At this, Zhinü waved a naked arm at Niulang. "I must've torn it upon removing my gown for my bath. What should I do?"

"I will help you," Niulang vowed. "You'll not be alone."

Zhinü heard the kindness in Niulang's voice, and found herself drawn to him, as she had been when she watched him from the Sky. When she looked into his eyes, she saw her future with him reflected in his black pupils. It was a scintillating and happy one.

The future I see in Niulang's eyes is too temptingly

good to give up, Zhinü thought to herself. *I will risk my parents' anger, break my promises to them and be chastised for my unfilial ways, and stay on Earth with him for as long as I can.*

To Niulang, she said, "You inspired me to come to Earth, and here I will stay. I want this life with you that I see before me."

And so, despite knowing the consequences of her decision, Zhinü made up her mind to remain on Earth to be with Niulang.

Niulang helped Zhinü on to Niuniu's broad back before clambering on to the buffalo himself. With Niulang behind her, Zhinü rode on the buffalo like a princess riding her chariot, towards her new home.

"One day, you will take us to the stars, Niuniu," Zhinü said, patting the buffalo on its head. "But for now I'll remain on Earth with you and Niulang."

Zhinü's shiny touch turned Niuniu into a magical buffalo. Instead of lumbering, Niuniu flew the couple home to start their new lives together.

Thus, Zhinü packed away her gossamer gown with its torn sleeve, and she soon forgot about her starlit life. And so the years passed in the twinkle of an eye.

*

Niulang and his wife, Zhinü, became a beloved couple, known for their kindness and compassion. The couple had two beautiful twin daughters, whom Niulang doted on and Zhinü loved with all her heart. To make a living, Zhinü wove beautiful cloth that she sold to dressmakers in the city, while Niulang and Niuniu worked the land, providing food for their family and others.

Life was peaceful until one day, out of the blue, the skies darkened. Bolts of lightning struck, and thunder rumbled angrily.

It was the Jade Emperor in a fit of rage. He had discovered Zhinü's ruse, and he was angry that one of his daughters had managed to trick him for so long. In a burst of temper, he reached down to Earth with outstretched arms to snatch Zhinü from her loom while her two daughters slept.

"How dare you be so insolent, Daughter?" the Jade Emperor thundered. "A goddess can never be married to a man! You have broken the rules of Heaven! And to think that your mother had covered for you all this time."

Zhinü held on to her loom to prevent the Jade Emperor from dragging her away. She fought her father with all the human might that she had, but the Jade Emperor, being a god, was far stronger than her. Seeing that there was nothing she could do physically, Zhinü changed tactics and begged him to let her stay.

"Father, please! Take pity on my children. They need their mother," Zhinü pleaded.

This angered the Jade Emperor further because he had no time for his half-human granddaughters. He would have preferred if they were grandsons, but, regardless, celestial rules were celestial rules.

Niulang came home to find his daughters crying in distress for their mother. He discovered his wife's loom broken in two. The cloth that Zhinü was weaving had turned translucent, reminding Niulang of her gossamer gown. Immediately, he understood what had happened.

Niuniu, with his magical powers, was now able not only to fly but to speak. "Niulang, climb on to my broad back, and I will take you to Zhinü."

Just as Zhinü had once predicted, Niuniu flew to the stars – with Niulang and the twins on his back.

But when they neared the stargate, the entrance to the Jade Emperor's celestial kingdom, they were barred from entering by two palace guards. The Jade

Emperor heard of Niulang's arrival, and in his fury he struck the sky with lightning so bright and so strong that it made Niuniu stumble backwards. Loud rolls of thunder boomed after it, and the twin girls woke up from their nap in fright.

Zhinü watched helplessly behind the palace gates as the Jade Emperor made a slash across the sky, creating a milky river that separated her from Niulang for all eternity.

Seeing what her husband had done, and witnessing her daughter in such despair, Xiwangmu Niangniang persuaded the Jade Emperor to have pity on their seventh child. "A husband needs his wife, and the children need their mother. Let the couple meet once a year," she pleaded.

Now, the Jade Emperor loved his wife very much. He did not like it that his actions had made her cry out in desperation. Heeding her, he calmed down, and the thundering in the sky subsided.

The Jade Emperor contemplated what his wife had said. He was still angry that his rules had been broken, but he also knew that even he, the Heavenly Grandfather, Supreme Ruler of the Celestial Skies, needed his wife, Xiwangmu Niangniang. He especially needed her for her wisdom. And hence, he called for a tittering of magpies to gather in his garden.

"Magpies, I command you to form a bridge across the milky river that I've created," said the Jade Emperor. "You are birds of happiness, and I want you to make Niulang and Zhinü happy for one day in the year."

And so it was that the earthly Niulang and the heavenly Zhinü were allowed to meet once a year, on the seventh day of the seventh lunar month, crossing the Milky Way with their enduring love. And from that day onwards, magpies have come to be symbols of happiness for the people of East Asia.

ABOUT THE AUTHOR

Eva Wong Nava is a child of the diaspora. She lives between two worlds, straddling the eastern and western hemispheres. Her ancestors braved monsoon winds sailing from the Middle Kingdom to Southeast Asia in the nineteenth century. When the winds changed, her relatives set sail again. This time for colder climes, fending hail storms to settle in Europe during the twentieth century. She comes from a family of storytellers, and that was how she got to know many of the stories in this anthology. When she grew up, she became a writer, and she writes stories that are filled with adventure and magic for children. Eva believes that children are the most important readers in the world, and stories are windows to other worlds. When not writing, she can be found in art museums and galleries, waiting for the next artefact or artwork to inspire a story.

OTHER FOLKTALES, MYTHS AND LEGENDS

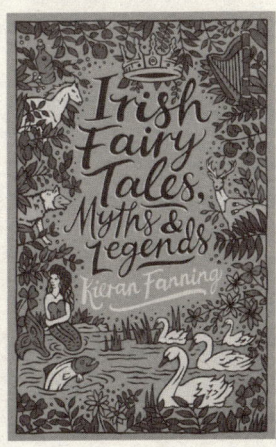
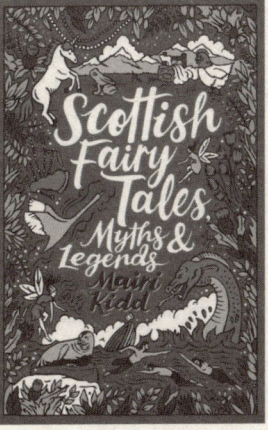